SIFT Study Guide 2024-2025

Unlock Your Potential with Comprehensive Study Materials, Proven Strategies, 2 Full-Length Practice Tests, and Expert Tips for the SIFT Exam

Test Treasure Publication

COPYRIGHT

Unauthorized use or duplication of this material without express and written permission from this site's owner and/or author is strictly prohibited. Excerpts and links may be used, provided that full and clear credit is given to Test Treasure Publication with appropriate and specific direction to the original content.

Trademarks

All trademarks, service marks, and trade names used within this website and Test Treasure Publication's products are proprietary to Test Treasure Publication or other respective owners that have granted Test Treasure Publication the right and license to use such intellectual property.

Disclaimer

While every effort has been made to ensure the accuracy and completeness of the information contained in our products, Test Treasure Publication assumes no responsibility for errors, omissions, or contradictory interpretation of the subject matter herein. All information is provided "as is" without warranty of any kind.

Governing Law

This website is controlled by Test Treasure Publication from our offices located in the state of California, USA. It can be accessed by most countries around the world. As each country has laws that may differ from those of California, by accessing our website, you agree that the statutes and laws of California, without regard to the conflict of laws and the United Nations Convention on the International Sales of Goods, will apply to all matters relating to the use of this website and the purchase of any products or services through this site.

Contents

INTRODUCTION

Welcome to the **SIFT Exam Study Guide 2024-2025**, a resource designed to help you excel in the Selection Instrument for Flight Training (SIFT) exam and achieve your goal of joining the elite ranks of U.S. Army aviation. This guide is more than just a study aid—it's a structured path to building the knowledge, skills, and confidence you need to succeed.

The SIFT exam is a pivotal step in becoming an Army Aviator, as it assesses both your academic aptitude and your potential to excel in challenging aviation training. With this in mind, we've meticulously crafted this guide to ensure you are fully prepared, equipped with all the tools necessary to perform your best on test day.

What This Guide Covers

This book offers a **comprehensive breakdown of the SIFT exam**, organized to cover each major section:

1. **Army Aviation Information**
   This section delves into key concepts such as aerodynamics, flight controls, weight and balance, and basic maneuvers—essential knowledge for aspiring Army aviators.

2. Reading Comprehension

We provide strategic techniques to improve your reading comprehension skills, essential for understanding complex texts quickly and accurately.

3. Math Skills

From basic operations to geometry, this section builds a solid foundation in mathematics, with practice problems tailored to match SIFT standards.

4. Mechanical Comprehension

This section covers essential mechanical principles, including kinetics, work and energy, and the fundamentals of machines and magnetism, to enhance your understanding of the physics related to aviation.

5. Practice Tests with Detailed Explanations

To give you a realistic feel of the actual exam, this guide includes two full-length practice tests, each consisting of 100 questions. Every answer is accompanied by detailed explanations to help you understand the reasoning and methodology behind each solution.

Why This Guide Will Help You Succeed

The **SIFT Exam Study Guide 2024-2025** is designed with a student-centered approach, offering a step-by-step guide that simplifies complex topics and enhances learning. We've included the following features to help maximize your study time and boost your confidence:

- **Strategic Insights and Study Schedules**: Find actionable study schedules that align with your time constraints and recommended strategies for each section, allowing you to manage your preparation efficiently.

- **Expert-Verified Content**: Each topic and question in this guide has been thoroughly researched and verified by experts to ensure relevance and accuracy.

- **Detailed Answer Explanations**: With clear explanations provided for each practice question, you can develop a deeper understanding of each subject and identify areas for improvement.

Achieving Your Aviation Dreams

Our goal is to empower you with knowledge and confidence as you embark on this journey toward a career in military aviation. The SIFT exam is challenging, but with dedication, hard work, and the right resources, success is within your reach.

Thank you for choosing this study guide as part of your preparation. We're excited to be part of your journey and look forward to seeing you soar to new heights. Let's get started and bring your dream of becoming an Army Aviator closer to reality!

BRIEF OVERVIEW OF THE EXAM AND ITS IMPORTANCE

The **Selection Instrument for Flight Training (SIFT)** exam is a vital step in the journey of becoming an Army Aviator. Administered by the **U.S. Army**, this exam evaluates a candidate's aptitude for aviation training, covering areas such as mathematical and mechanical skills, reading comprehension, and aviation knowledge. Success on the SIFT exam is essential, as it not only measures your foundational abilities but also predicts your potential to excel in the rigorous and demanding environment of Army aviation training.

Why the SIFT Exam Matters

The SIFT exam serves as a comprehensive filter, ensuring that only candidates with the essential skills and knowledge are selected for Army aviation training. This exam is more than just a test of your current understanding; it assesses your ability to grasp complex concepts and quickly adapt to new learning—qualities that are crucial for any successful Army Aviator. Passing the SIFT is an indication of your readiness to meet the high standards of Army aviation.

Exam Pattern

The SIFT exam is structured to evaluate multiple skill areas critical to aviation training. The test is **computer-based** and divided into seven distinct sections, each focusing on specific competencies.

Exam Sections

1. **Simple Drawings** – Tests spatial perception and attention to detail.

2. **Hidden Figures** – Assesses visual acuity and the ability to recognize patterns.

3. **Army Aviation Information** – Measures knowledge of aerodynamics, aviation principles, and aircraft operations.

4. **Reading Comprehension** – Evaluates your ability to read and understand complex texts efficiently.

5. **Mathematics Skills** – Covers basic arithmetic, algebra, and geometry essential for aviation tasks.

6. **Mechanical Comprehension** – Tests understanding of physics concepts, including mechanics and electricity.

7. **Spatial Apperception** – Assesses the ability to visualize and interpret three-dimensional objects and scenarios.

Each section is designed to evaluate distinct skills, contributing to a well-rounded assessment of a candidate's readiness for aviation training.

Number of Questions and Timing

The SIFT exam contains **100 questions in total**, spread across the seven sections. Each section has a specific number of questions and an allotted time:

- **Simple Drawings**: 50 questions – 2 minutes each

- **Hidden Figures**: 50 questions – 2 minutes each

- **Army Aviation Information**: 40 questions – 30 minutes

- **Reading Comprehension**: 20 questions – 30 minutes

- **Mathematics Skills**: 30 questions – 40 minutes

- **Mechanical Comprehension**: 25 questions – 15 minutes

- **Spatial Apperception**: 25 questions – 10 minutes

The total testing time is approximately **2 hours and 40 minutes**, but test-takers should be prepared for slight variations in timing across sections.

Scoring and Passing Requirements

The SIFT exam is scored on a scale from **20 to 80**, with **40 being the minimum passing score**. However, achieving a higher score significantly enhances your competitiveness as a candidate. A strong performance on the SIFT demonstrates not only competence in aviation-related knowledge but also readiness for the demands of aviation training.

Your score on the SIFT is final—candidates are allowed only two attempts, and the second attempt can only occur after a wait period of 180 days. Failing to achieve a passing score after two attempts disqualifies candidates from pursuing an Army aviation career.

Administered By

The **U.S. Army** administers the SIFT exam at authorized Army Education Centers and testing facilities across the United States. Candidates should contact their local Army recruiter or education center to schedule the test. Only authorized testing centers are equipped to deliver the computer-based exam in a secure environment.

Final Thoughts on the SIFT Exam's Importance

Passing the SIFT is a critical milestone for aspiring Army Aviators. This exam not only tests foundational skills but also reflects a candidate's readiness for the challenging path ahead. A high score on the SIFT increases your chances of selection and sets you on the path toward a rewarding career in Army aviation. This study guide is designed to give you a thorough preparation, equipping you with the knowledge and strategies needed to tackle each section confidently and achieve a competitive score.

DETAILED CONTENT REVIEW

This **SIFT Exam Study Guide 2024-2025** is structured to provide comprehensive, in-depth coverage of each of the seven sections of the SIFT exam. Each chapter of the guide is carefully organized to build your knowledge, reinforce your skills, and boost your confidence for test day. Below, you'll find a detailed overview of each section's content, covering key concepts, practice questions, and strategic insights.

Section 1: Simple Drawings

This section evaluates your **attention to detail** and ability to **discern visual differences**. In this part of the guide, you'll find:

- Techniques for quickly identifying differences between similar drawings.

- Practice questions that mirror actual SIFT exam visuals.

- Tips for time management, as each question in this section is time-sensitive.

Key Topics Covered:

- Pattern recognition

- Visual perception exercises

- Speed and accuracy strategies

Section 2: Hidden Figures

The Hidden Figures section measures your **visual acuity** and **pattern recognition**. This part of the guide includes:

- Exercises to improve your ability to spot hidden shapes within complex images.

- Step-by-step explanations of practice problems to help you grasp common hidden figure patterns.

- Visual drills to enhance speed in recognizing shapes accurately under timed conditions.

Key Topics Covered:

- Shape identification

- Figure-ground perception

- Rapid recognition techniques

Section 3: Army Aviation Information

This section is pivotal for aspiring Army Aviators, as it tests your **foundational knowledge of aviation principles**. Our content review provides:

- Detailed explanations of core aviation topics like **aerodynamics**, **flight controls**, **weight and balance**, and **basic maneuvers**.

- Diagrams and illustrations to clarify complex concepts and principles.

- Practice questions with answer explanations that deepen your understanding of aviation theory.

Key Topics Covered:

- **Aerodynamics**: Lift, drag, thrust, and weight

- **Flight Controls**: Ailerons, rudder, and elevator functions

- **Weight and Balance**: Understanding load distribution

- **Basic Maneuvers**: Types of turns, descents, and climbs

Section 4: Reading Comprehension

The Reading Comprehension section assesses your ability to **quickly read and understand complex texts**. This guide equips you with:

- Proven strategies to identify main ideas, supporting details, and infer meaning.

- Tips on how to approach each passage to maximize accuracy and efficiency.

- Practice passages with detailed answer explanations that simulate actual exam questions.

Key Topics Covered:

- Identifying main ideas and supporting details

- Making inferences

- Understanding vocabulary in context

- Improving reading speed and comprehension accuracy

Section 5: Mathematics Skills

This section tests core **mathematical abilities essential for aviation**. The guide provides:

- A thorough review of essential math skills, from arithmetic to geometry.

- Step-by-step practice problems with explanations to clarify complex calculations.

- Quick-reference tables and tips for efficient problem-solving under time constraints.

Key Topics Covered:

- **Operations**: Addition, subtraction, multiplication, and division

- **Positive and Negative Numbers**: Understanding integers

- **Factors and Multiples**: Prime factorization and least common multiples

- **Systems of Equations**: Solving for variables in two-variable equations

- **Polynomial Algebra**: Simplifying expressions and solving polynomials

- **Solving Quadratic Equations**: Using the quadratic formula

- **Basic Geometry**: Perimeter, area, and properties of shapes

Section 6: Mechanical Comprehension

The Mechanical Comprehension section is crucial for assessing your grasp of **basic physics concepts** related to mechanics and aviation. This part of the guide includes:

- Clear explanations of fundamental mechanical concepts, from kinetic energy to magnetism.

- Diagrams and visual aids to illustrate mechanical principles.

- Practice questions with in-depth explanations to improve problem-solving skills.

Key Topics Covered:

- **Kinetics**: Motion, force, and acceleration

- **Work and Energy**: Concepts of work, kinetic, and potential energy

- **Machines**: Levers, pulleys, and gears

- **Momentum and Impulse**: Conservation of momentum

- **Fluids**: Buoyancy, pressure, and flow principles

- **Heat Transfer**: Conduction, convection, and radiation

- **Optics**: Light properties and lenses

- **Electricity and Magnetism**: Electric circuits, magnetic fields, and electromagnetism

Section 7: Spatial Apperception

Spatial Apperception tests your **ability to visualize and interpret three-dimensional objects and scenarios**. This guide prepares you with:

- Techniques for enhancing spatial awareness and visualizing objects from different perspectives.

- Practice exercises with illustrations to help you interpret and manipulate spatial scenarios quickly and accurately.

- Real-world applications of spatial skills to improve your understanding of how they relate to aviation.

Key Topics Covered:

- **3D Visualization**: Understanding perspective changes and rotations

- **Spatial Orientation**: Interpreting various aircraft positions and angles

- **Mental Rotation**: Developing skills to visualize object rotations accurately

Full-Length Practice Tests

To help you solidify your knowledge and apply what you've learned, this guide includes **two full-length practice tests**, each with **100 questions** that span all exam sections. Each question is followed by:

- Detailed answer explanations to clarify concepts and address common pitfalls.

- Performance analysis suggestions to help you focus on areas where you need improvement.

Final Thoughts

This **Detailed Content Review** gives you the tools you need to build a strong foundation in each area covered by the SIFT exam. By following this structured guide and working through the practice questions, you'll be well-prepared to face each section with confidence and achieve a high score on the SIFT exam.

STUDY SCHEDULES AND PLANNING ADVICE

Preparing for the SIFT exam requires a well-structured study plan that maximizes both time and efficiency. With diverse sections testing various skills—from math to mechanical comprehension and spatial reasoning—having a clear study schedule will help ensure that you're well-prepared for every part of the exam. Below, you'll find sample study schedules for different timelines, along with key planning advice to guide you through a successful preparation journey.

Step 1: Assess Your Timeline and Commitments

Before creating your study schedule, determine how much time you have before your test date and assess your current level of familiarity with the SIFT exam material. If you're taking the exam within a month, a more intensive schedule will be necessary. For those with two or more months, a slower-paced, comprehensive review is achievable. Here are three sample study timelines to consider:

- **1-Month Intensive Plan**: For candidates with only four weeks to prepare.

- **2-Month Balanced Plan**: For candidates with roughly eight weeks.

- **3-Month Comprehensive Plan**: For those with a full 12-week preparation period.

Each plan is tailored to cover all the material effectively within the available time.

Sample Study Schedules

1-Month Intensive Plan

For students with only 4 weeks until their exam, daily dedication and focus are essential. Aim to cover one main topic each week and reserve the final week for review and practice exams.

- **Week 1**: Army Aviation Information & Simple Drawings

    - **Days 1-3**: Army Aviation Information—study aerodynamics, flight controls, weight and balance, and basic maneuvers.

    - **Days 4-7**: Simple Drawings—practice identifying differences and work on timing.

- **Week 2**: Reading Comprehension & Mathematics Skills

    - **Days 1-3**: Reading Comprehension—focus on identifying main ideas and practicing reading strategies.

    - **Days 4-7**: Mathematics Skills—review operations, positive and negative numbers, factors and multiples, and basic geometry.

- **Week 3**: Mechanical Comprehension & Spatial Apperception

    - **Days 1-3**: Mechanical Comprehension—study kinetics, work/energy, machines, and fluids.

- ○ **Days 4-7**: Spatial Apperception—practice 3D visualization and interpreting spatial changes.

- **Week 4**: Review and Full-Length Practice Tests

  - ○ **Days 1-3**: Comprehensive review of all sections; focus on weaker areas.

  - ○ **Days 4-7**: Take full-length practice tests, analyze results, and review mistakes.

2-Month Balanced Plan

With 8 weeks, you can adopt a more moderate pace, focusing on one to two sections per week. This allows for more detailed review and spaced repetition.

- **Weeks 1-2**: Army Aviation Information & Simple Drawings

- **Weeks 3-4**: Reading Comprehension & Mathematics Skills

- **Weeks 5-6**: Mechanical Comprehension & Spatial Apperception

- **Weeks 7-8**: Review, Full-Length Practice Tests, and Analysis

In this schedule, dedicate 3-4 days per week to learning new material and 1-2 days for reviewing previously covered content. The last two weeks should be reserved for comprehensive review and taking practice tests to solidify your knowledge.

3-Month Comprehensive Plan

With 12 weeks available, you have ample time for in-depth study and gradual review of each topic. This plan is ideal for students who can dedicate a few hours per week without the pressure of cramming.

- **Weeks 1-2**: Army Aviation Information

- **Weeks 3-4**: Simple Drawings

- **Weeks 5-6**: Reading Comprehension

- **Weeks 7-8**: Mathematics Skills

- **Weeks 9-10**: Mechanical Comprehension

- **Weeks 11-12**: Spatial Apperception, Final Review, and Practice Tests

Spend 2-3 days each week studying a section, and use weekends or spare days for practice questions or review. In the last month, shift focus to practice tests and timed exercises to enhance your exam readiness.

Key Study Tips and Planning Advice

1. Prioritize Your Weaker Areas

While reviewing all sections is essential, spend extra time on areas where you feel less confident. Regularly test yourself with practice questions to monitor your progress and adjust your focus as needed.

2. Use Active Learning Techniques

Active learning techniques—such as taking notes, summarizing information in your own words, and teaching concepts to someone else—can significantly improve retention. Incorporate flashcards, diagrams, and self-quizzing to reinforce complex topics.

3. Practice with Timed Exercises

The SIFT exam is timed, so it's important to work on speed and accuracy. Regularly practice under timed conditions, especially for sections like **Simple Drawings** and **Hidden Figures**, where quick identification is crucial. Time yourself to become accustomed to working within the exam's pace.

4. Review and Reflect

After each practice test or quiz, review your mistakes thoroughly. Note down any recurring errors or concepts that need further review. Reflection and correction are key to avoiding similar mistakes on the actual exam.

5. Use Visualization Techniques for Spatial Apperception

For the Spatial Apperception section, practice visualizing 3D objects from various perspectives. Visualization exercises, such as mentally rotating objects or sketching perspectives, can be incredibly beneficial for this section.

6. Take Regular Breaks to Avoid Burnout

While it's essential to stay consistent, regular breaks are also crucial. Study for 25-50 minutes, then take a short break to recharge. This approach, often called the Pomodoro Technique, can help maintain focus and prevent burnout, especially during intensive study sessions.

7. Simulate Test Conditions Before Exam Day

In the final week, aim to replicate the test environment as closely as possible. Take full-length practice tests in a quiet space without interruptions. Use only the allotted time for each section and follow the order of the actual exam to build endurance and reduce test-day anxiety.

Final Words on Study Planning

Effective preparation for the SIFT exam is about consistency, strategic focus, and smart time management. Whether you have one month or three, a well-structured study plan and diligent practice will build the confidence and skills needed to achieve a high score. Stick to your schedule, stay motivated, and remember that each step brings you closer to your goal of becoming an Army Aviator. Good luck, and let this study guide be your trusted companion on the path to success!

FREQUENTLY ASKED QUESTIONS

This section addresses common questions about the SIFT exam and the best ways to prepare using this study guide. Understanding these FAQs will help you feel more confident and informed as you approach your exam preparation.

1. What is the SIFT Exam, and why is it important?

The Selection Instrument for Flight Training (SIFT) exam is a critical test used by the U.S. Army to assess the aptitude of candidates aspiring to become Army Aviators. The exam evaluates a wide range of skills, including mathematics, mechanical comprehension, spatial awareness, and aviation knowledge. Passing the SIFT exam is essential, as it demonstrates that you possess the foundational skills needed to succeed in Army aviation training.

2. How many sections are on the SIFT exam, and what do they cover?

The SIFT exam consists of seven sections, each designed to test a specific skill set:

- **Simple Drawings**: Identifying differences in shapes and images.

- **Hidden Figures**: Recognizing hidden shapes within complex patterns.

- **Army Aviation Information**: Knowledge of aviation principles, aerodynamics, flight controls, and basic maneuvers.

- **Reading Comprehension**: Ability to understand complex passages and answer questions.

- **Mathematics Skills**: Includes arithmetic, algebra, and geometry.

- **Mechanical Comprehension**: Tests understanding of physics concepts relevant to aviation.

- **Spatial Apperception**: Assesses spatial awareness and 3D visualization skills.

Each section contributes to a comprehensive assessment of your suitability for Army aviation training.

3. What score do I need to pass the SIFT exam?

The SIFT exam is scored on a scale from **20 to 80**, with a minimum passing score of **40**. However, achieving a higher score is recommended to enhance your competitiveness and improve your chances of selection. Remember that you are allowed only two attempts at the SIFT exam, so thorough preparation is essential.

4. How should I use this study guide to prepare for the SIFT exam?

This study guide is organized to cover each section of the SIFT exam in detail. Begin by reviewing the **Detailed Content Review** for each section to understand the material. Use the **practice questions** provided to test your knowledge, and focus on understanding the **answer explanations** to learn from any mistakes. In the final weeks before the exam, take the **full-length practice tests** under timed conditions to build your test-taking skills and confidence.

5. How much time should I dedicate to studying each week?

The amount of study time depends on your familiarity with the topics and the time you have before the test. On average, 8-12 hours per week is recommended for comprehensive preparation. Refer to the **Study Schedules and Planning Advice** section in this guide for suggested timelines, whether you have 1 month, 2 months, or 3 months to prepare.

6. What are the best strategies for the Reading Comprehension section?

For the Reading Comprehension section, focus on understanding the main idea, identifying supporting details, and making inferences. Practice reading quickly yet accurately, and avoid getting bogged down by complex vocabulary. This guide provides strategic tips and sample passages to help you build your reading skills.

7. Is there a specific way to approach the Mechanical Comprehension section?

Yes, the Mechanical Comprehension section covers concepts from physics, including mechanics, electricity, and optics. Start by reviewing the foundational principles for each topic, then practice solving problems to understand how these principles are applied. Visual aids and diagrams in this guide can help clarify concepts, making it easier to grasp the material.

8. How can I improve my spatial reasoning skills for the Spatial Apperception section?

Improving spatial reasoning involves practice and visualization. This guide provides exercises that train you to visualize and interpret 3D objects and rotations. Practice by mentally rotating shapes or sketching them from different angles. Spatial awareness is a skill that improves with consistent practice, so dedicate time to this section regularly.

9. What if I need extra help with math concepts?

This guide covers essential math topics, including arithmetic, algebra, and geometry. If you need extra support, consider using additional math resources, such as online tutorials, math apps, or review books. Practice regularly to build confidence, and remember that the answer explanations in this guide provide step-by-step breakdowns of each solution.

10. How can I manage my time effectively during the exam?

Time management is crucial for the SIFT exam, as each section has a specific time limit. Practice answering questions under timed conditions to build speed and accuracy. For sections like Simple Drawings and Hidden Figures, work quickly and move on if you're unsure of an answer. The more you practice under exam-like conditions, the more comfortable you'll become with pacing yourself.

11. Are there any strategies for reducing test anxiety on exam day?

Yes, managing test anxiety can help you perform your best. Try these tips:

- **Practice deep breathing** to stay calm.

- **Visualize success** before the test.

- **Get adequate rest** the night before the exam.

- **Arrive early** at the testing center to avoid feeling rushed.

- **Review your study guide** briefly before entering the exam to refresh your memory.

Taking practice tests in this guide under realistic conditions can also help reduce anxiety, as it familiarizes you with the test environment.

12. What happens if I don't pass the SIFT on my first attempt?

If you don't pass the SIFT exam on your first attempt, you may retake it after a 180-day waiting period. You are only allowed **two attempts** at the SIFT, so if you don't pass on the second try, you will not be able to pursue an Army aviation career. This makes careful preparation essential to increase your chances of passing on the first attempt.

13. Can I take the SIFT exam if I'm not in the Army yet?

Yes, the SIFT exam is open to both current Army personnel and civilians interested in becoming Army Aviators. If you're not yet enlisted, reach out to a recruiter to learn about the requirements for scheduling the SIFT exam and to confirm your eligibility for an Army aviation career.

Final Advice

Preparing for the SIFT exam is a significant undertaking, but with dedication, strategic preparation, and effective use of this guide, success is within reach. Remember that consistent study, regular practice, and careful review of each section's content will help you build the knowledge and confidence needed to excel. Good luck, and we wish you every success on your journey to becoming an Army Aviator!

Section 1: The Army Aviation Information Test

1.1 Aerodynamics

Alright, folks, let's dive headfirst into the wild world of aerodynamics. You ready? Good, 'cause we're about to unravel the secrets behind lift, that magical force that lets planes soar high above the ground.

You see, lift is like the ultimate mind-bender. It's what makes all those planes look like they're defying gravity, floating gracefully through the sky. And to get why lift is such a big deal, we gotta get acquainted with Bernoulli's principle, the backbone of aerodynamics.

So, imagine this: we're on a ship, sailing smoothly through the sea of knowledge, with a gentle breeze guiding us. And this breeze is all about the delicate balance between pressure and velocity that creates lift. It's like a dance, a beautiful choreography that gives aircraft the ability to fly. And we're gonna dig deep into Bernoulli's principle, peeling back its layers to uncover its jaw-dropping secrets.

But hold on tight, 'cause we can't just focus on lift alone. Oh no, there's also this sneaky force called drag that loves to play spoiler. Drag's like that annoying little brother who tries to slow us down, making it harder for us to reach greater speeds and efficiency. But hey, no worries! Armed with knowledge, we're gonna subdue this pesky drag and make it work for us.

Now, let's take a step-by-step journey through the world of drag. We've got three main players here: form drag, skin friction drag, and interference drag. Each one has its own unique role in this crazy game of aerodynamics. And we won't stop there! We'll go in-depth into the factors that mess with drag, from the shape and size of an aircraft to the texture of its outside. Understanding the ins and outs of drag will help us streamline our path through the sky, reducing resistance and maximizing efficiency.

Next up, we've got thrust, the force that propels us forward like a turbocharged super engine. Thrust is like our trusty steed, helping us conquer massive distances and explore the vastness of the skies. We'll tackle the different sources of thrust, like those powerful jet engines, sturdy propellers, speedy turbofans, and badass rockets. These bad boys are engineering marvels, harnessing unimaginable power to make us fly.

Now, let's shift gears a bit and talk about equilibrium. This is all about balance, my friends, what keeps an aircraft stable and allows us to fly with control. From the center of gravity to stability and control, we're diving deep into the mechanics of flight dynamics. Get ready to marvel at the interplay of forces that lets pilots maneuver their planes with finesse and skill.

And just when you thought things couldn't get any cooler, we're venturing into the mesmerizing realm of fluid dynamics. Here, we see physics colliding with the graceful movements of fluids. It's like watching a mesmerizing dance, where forces and vortices shape the behavior of air and water alike.

So, here's the deal, my fellow adventurers. At Test Treasure Publication, we're your trusty comrades on this exhilarating journey. We're gonna guide you through the twists and turns of this knowledge maze, igniting your passion for mastering the art of aerodynamics. Our mission is to empower you, equip you with the insight and understanding to conquer any challenge that dares cross your path, so you can reach for the stars.

So buckle up, my dear reader, 'cause together, we're embarking on an epic adventure through the captivating world of aerodynamics. It's where physics and engineering shake hands, creating the wonders of flight. This is the place where dreams take flight, where the sky is not the limit anymore. Welcome to this breathtaking world, where science and the magic of flight come together in perfect harmony.

1.2 Flight Controls

Have you ever wondered what it feels like to take control of the sky? To have the power to ascend or descend, gracefully navigating the vast expanse above us? Well, my friend, at Test Treasure Publication, we understand the significance of mastering the art of flight controls. So, let's dive into the wonderland of flight controls, shall we? We'll uncover the complexities that lie beneath these seemingly simple mechanisms.

Now, picture this: You're in the cockpit, ready to conquer the skies. The first control we encounter is the elevator. It's this horizontal surface hinged to the tail of the aircraft, and it's responsible for the nose's vertical movement, or what we call "pitch." So, basically, when you want to climb higher or descend gracefully, you just manipulate that control column, and voila! The elevator responds obediently, giving you absolute authority over your altitude.

Next up, we have the ailerons. These fantastic components are attached to the wings, near the fuselage. They're like a pair of wings for your wings! They help you roll in either direction, giving you control over your aircraft's direction. It's like riding a bike, but in the sky! All you need to do is delicately maneuver that control wheel, and the ailerons will dance in perfect harmony, gifting you with precision and grace in executing turns and fancy maneuvers.

And let's not forget about the rudder, the real MVP located at the tail of the aircraft. This powerful control surface allows the aircraft to rotate around its vertical axis, resulting in what we call "yaw" motion. So, when you move those rudder pedals with expertise, you magically influence the direction in which the nose points. It's like painting in the sky, adding a touch of finesse and mastery to your flight.

But hold on, there's more to explore! Let me introduce you to the secondary control surfaces. These bad boys amplify the effectiveness of the primary controls, giving you even more control over your aircraft's behavior. They're like the cherry on the cake.

First, we have the leading-edge devices, like the leading-edge flaps and slats. These cool additions transform your wings, making them more efficient and enhancing your aircraft's ability to generate lift and control its speed during approach and landing. It's like having an extra set of wings, but cooler! You just need to expertly manipulate those switches or levers, adapting your aircraft to the ever-changing demands of flight.

Now, let's talk about the trailing-edge devices. We have the flaps, near the trailing edge of the wings, which allow you to modify the surface area of your wings. This comes in handy when you need to fly at lower speeds or achieve shorter takeoff and landing distances. And then we have spoilers, these smart augmenters that prevent the wings from generating lift in specific sections. They help you reduce your speed and facilitate a controlled descent. It's like having a built-in brake system for the sky!

Oh, wait, there's another set of heroes we can't overlook—the trim controls! These unsung mechanisms are often overshadowed by their more famous friends. But, they play a crucial role in maintaining constant control forces and counteracting any imbalances in the aircraft. Think of them as the best buddies who lighten your load and keep you focused. With a nifty manipulation of those trim tabs, you achieve a state of equilibrium, granting you enhanced control over the primary flight controls.

And hey, we can't ignore the game-changing technological advancements in the aviation industry! From fly-by-wire systems to digital avionics, the modern era has transformed the way we interact with our aircraft. The pilot's capabilities have expanded thanks to sophisticated electronic interfaces and computer algorithms. But hey, it also means we need to understand how humans and machines play together in this sky-high realm.

So, my friend, are you ready to embark on this epic journey? Test Treasure Publication invites you to join us on this voyage of discovery. Together, we'll unravel the mysteries of flight controls and empower you to soar to new heights of mastery and understanding. Trust me, it's going to be one heck of an adventure!

1.3 Weight and Balance

Welcome, my fellow aviators, to the fascinating world of weight and balance. Today, we're diving headfirst into this crucial aspect of the aviation industry. Buckle up, because we're about to embark on a thrilling journey of understanding.

First things first, let's talk about what weight and balance really mean. Picture this: you're soaring through the skies, feeling the rush of the wind against your face. But wait, what if the weight distribution in your aircraft is all messed up? Trust me, that's not a situation you want to find yourself in. That's why we need to have a deep understanding of weight and balance to ensure safe and efficient flight operations.

Now, let's get into the nitty-gritty, shall we? We're going to unravel the fundamental concepts that underpin this whole discipline. From the definition of weight and balance to the significance of aircraft loading, we'll cover it all. And don't worry, we'll make sure this isn't just a boring physics class. We're going to explore the effects of center of gravity on flight stability and maneuverability, using engaging illustrations and real-world examples. So, get ready to grasp the importance of maintaining proper weight distribution for a safe and controlled flight experience.

Okay, let's move on to the really interesting stuff. This is where things start to get intense. We're diving into a world where intricate factors come into play, impacting the weight and balance of an aircraft. We're talking passengers, fuel, cargo, and equipment. Each component has a role to play in the overall weight distribution and center of gravity. Can you imagine how these factors shape the stability of an aircraft during flight? It's like a delicate dance, my friends. But with our comprehensive guide, you'll gain a deep appreciation for the dynamic interplay of these elements and how they affect the performance of the aircraft.

Now, let's put our knowledge to the test. It's time to roll up our sleeves and get practical. We'll guide you through step-by-step weight and balance calculations, so you can determine the weight, balance, and center of gravity of an aircraft. This is where the rubber meets the road, my friends. You'll learn how to handle weight shifts during flight and calculate the maximum allowable takeoff weight. By the end of this section, you'll have the skills needed to maintain optimal aircraft performance.

Last but not least, we're taking a deep dive into the realm of weight and balance documentation. Yes, folks, paperwork is part of the game. But don't worry, it's not as daunting as it sounds. We're going to learn all about the various forms, charts, and documents required to record and communicate weight and balance information. We'll explore why these documents are so crucial in ensuring compliance with regulations and promoting safe flight operations. And we can't forget about those aircraft load manifests. They play a vital role in managing weight and balance efficiently. So get ready to develop the skills to accurately document and communicate weight and balance information, because professionalism and safety are at the heart of the aviation industry.

So, my friends, get ready to emerge from this chapter as competent and knowledgeable aviators. You'll navigate those skies with utmost precision and confidence. Our engaging discussions and practical examples have set the stage for you to excel in this critical aspect of aviation. Together, we're embarking on a remarkable journey through the intricacies of weight and balance. And trust me, once you discover the profound impact it has on the safety and performance of every flight, you'll never look at flying the same way again.

1.4 Basic Maneuvers

Let me tell you, mastering those basic maneuvers is the key to acing the SIFT exam. It's all about showing off your awareness of aircraft control and maneuverability. These maneuvers really put your flight planning, execution, and decision-making skills to the test.

As a pilot, you absolutely have to know your stuff when it comes to basic maneuvers. They lay the groundwork for all the fancy flying you'll be doing later on. Think of them as the building blocks of your aviation career.

So, let's dig into each maneuver in detail, exploring all the techniques, principles, and practical applications that come with them. By truly understanding each one, you'll not only rock the SIFT exam, but you'll also set yourself up with a solid foundation for your future in the sky.

First up, we've got straight and level flight. It's like the bread and butter of flying, maintaining a steady altitude and heading. This is the maneuver that keeps you in control and helps you navigate like a pro. We'll dive into all the nitty-gritty, from how control surfaces come into play to the importance of trim settings and instrument interpretation.

Next, we've got climbs and descents. Smoothly going up and down is absolutely crucial, because altitude can change on you at any moment. We'll talk all about power control, pitch adjustments, and airspeed management - everything you need to show off your ability to handle changes in altitude and control your ascent or descent.

Now, let's talk turns. Navigating the sky means being able to make those turns effectively. We'll explore all the different types of turns, from the coordinated to the uncoordinated. Banking the aircraft, controlling yaw, coordinating rudder and aileron usage - it's all gonna be covered. You want to be a master of turns? Well, this is where you'll build up those skills.

Alright, brace yourself, because it's slow flight time. This is when we really put your control to the test. We want to see you flying at those low speeds, demonstrating your mastery of control inputs and understanding of how the plane behaves. You'll learn all about power settings, control surfaces, and most importantly, how to prevent stalling.

Time for some excitement with steep turns. These bad boys are all about showing off your ability to navigate sharp, coordinated turns while dealing with the added forces. We'll teach you how to maintain that constant bank angle, coordinate those controls, and handle changes in altitude and airspeed. By mastering steep turns, you'll prove yourself to be the ultimate pilot in challenging conditions.

And last, but definitely not least, stalls and stall recovery. These situations are serious business - they can be dangerous if you don't know what you're doing. We'll make sure you can recognize stall indications, recover properly, and most importantly, keep control. You need to be able to handle unintentional stalls like a pro and show everyone that you've got what it takes to be a top-notch pilot.

By immersing yourself in all the ins and outs of each of these basic maneuvers, you'll build a solid foundation and hone the skills you need to rock the SIFT exam.

Remember, practice and understanding go hand in hand. With the guidance we're providing, you'll be totally ready to face the challenges of basic maneuvers with confidence and finesse. So, get ready to soar like never before!

1.5 Conclusion

Hey there! Can you believe the crazy journey we've been on, diving headfirst into the depths of history and unearthing all those mind-blowing moments that have shaped the world we live in? From brutal wars that tore nations apart to mind-boggling scientific breakthroughs that completely rocked our understanding of the universe – we've seen it all!

We've walked in the footsteps of these legendary leaders, some of them revered, some of them controversial, who've shaped the course of history by their actions and ideas. We've stood side by side with those courageous souls who fought tooth and nail for equality and justice, refusing to bow down to discrimination and oppression. And how awesome was it to witness those brilliant minds pushing the boundaries of discovery and innovation? It's like they were trying to smash through the glass ceiling of knowledge!

But let me tell you, this journey hasn't just been about memorizing facts and spitting out figures. Oh no, my friend, it's been a total transformation of your very being! Dive deep into these pages and you'll find yourself building the solid foundation upon which you'll conquer the world. You'll sharpen your critical thinking skills, learn how to dissect and interpret information like a boss, and form a deep understanding of how everything is connected.

But guess what? This ain't the end, my buddy. Nope, this is just the beginning of a wild and crazy adventure. Armed with the knowledge and skills you've acquired, you're all set to tackle any obstacle that comes your way. You're a force to be reckoned with – oozing confidence, determination, and an undying spirit.

But don't forget, this isn't where the road ends. No way! The world is your oyster, my friend, and it's up to you to grab it with both hands! As you set foot out into that big ol' world, let the lessons and insights you've gained be your guiding star. Let those stories of bravery and resilience fuel your fire as you reach for the stars. And let me tell you, the knowledge you've soaked up on these pages? It's the key that'll unlock all the doors to your success.

So, my incredible companion, Test Treasure Publication invites you to continue this extraordinary adventure. Let's light up the way to even bigger and better achievements. Let's celebrate the pursuit of knowledge as we navigate the roller-coaster ride that is education. Let us be your support system, your cheerleader, and your trusty guide as we dive into the next chapter of this epic journey together.

But for now, my fellow adventurer, I must bid you farewell. Remember, the real treasure lies not at the destination, but in every single moment of this crazy voyage. Embrace every challenge, savor every victory, and most importantly, never ever stop learning. Farewell, my fantastic friend, and may your path always be brightly illuminated by the incredible Test Treasure Publication.

Section 2: The Reading Comprehension Test

2.1 Strategies for Effective Reading

Effective reading is so much more than just deciphering words on a page. It's about really getting into the text, understanding it, and thinking critically about what it's saying. In today's crazy world, where everything is moving a mile a minute and our attention spans are shorter than ever, being able to read effectively is super important. Whether you're studying for a test or just trying to learn something new, getting good at reading is a game-changer.

So, in this chapter, we're gonna dive into a bunch of strategies that will level up your reading skills and turn you into a reading superstar. These strategies are gonna help you read faster, understand better, and remember and apply what you're reading. By using these techniques, you'll not only become a more efficient reader, but you'll also really connect with the material in a whole new way.

But before we get into the nitty-gritty of these strategies, let's talk about why effective reading is so dang important. When you're taking a test, time is usually not on your side. Being able to read quickly and really understand what you're reading is gonna make a huge difference in how well you do. It'll help you answer questions accurately and without wasting precious time. So, if you wanna ace that test, you gotta learn the strategies we're about to dive into.

But effective reading isn't just for tests, my friend. It's something that will make your everyday life better too. Think about it – from textbooks to news articles, from research papers to novels, we're always coming across written information that shapes how we see the world. So being able to read effectively lets us soak up all that knowledge, open up our minds, and make informed decisions. It's like a superpower that keeps on giving.

Now that we're all on the same page about why effective reading is so important, let's jump into the good stuff – the strategies that are gonna change the way you read forever. Each one of these strategies has been picked and designed to make your reading experience the best it can be. But here's the thing, my friend – practice and persistence are gonna be your BFFs on this journey to becoming a reading pro. So embrace these strategies, make them a part of who you are, and get ready to see a whole new side of yourself as you unleash your true reading potential.

Alright, enough talk – it's time to dive headfirst into the world of effective reading and discover the strategies that are gonna take you to places you never thought possible. Let's go!

2.2 Identifying Main Ideas and Supporting Details

Alright, my friend, don't you worry! In this chapter, we're diving deep into the art of uncovering main ideas and supporting details. It's like unlocking the treasure chest of understanding and comprehension. So, let's get ready for this journey and arm ourselves with the tools we need to unravel any text's complexities.

Step 1: Get to Know the Passage

Before we can uncover those main ideas and supporting details, we've got to acquaint ourselves with the passage at hand. It's not just a task to be done – think of it as an adventure waiting to happen. Immerse yourself in those words, and let their meaning soak into your brain. Soak up the context, feel the tone, and embrace the author's point of view. Only when we're fully engaged can we start to decode the heart of the passage.

Step 2: Spot the Topic Sentence

Think of the topic sentence like a guiding star in the night sky. It shines a light on the main idea of a paragraph, giving us a clue about the author's central message. Watch out for the opening sentence of each paragraph – that's where the key lies. Underline or highlight those topic sentences, because they're going to guide us through the maze of details.

Step 3: Follow the Road of Supporting Details

Once we've located those topic sentences, it's time for a quest to dig up the supporting details that strengthen those main ideas. Think of these details as the threads in a tapestry, adding depth and evidence to the author's claims. Look for facts, examples, statistics, or expert opinions – they'll shed light on those main ideas and strengthen the author's arguments.

Step 4: Separate the Main Ideas from Supporting Details

As we gather the puzzle pieces, we need to have a keen eye to tell the main ideas apart from the supporting details. A main idea is like a massive concept that covers the whole passage, while supporting details give evidence, examples, or explanations to back up that main idea. Imagine the main ideas as the pillars holding up a majestic building, and the supporting details as the bricks that make them strong. Pay attention to the importance and relevance of each piece of information, and think about how it contributes to the author's message.

Step 5: Unravel the Little Things

In the intricate web of language, there are often surprises hiding below the surface. Keep an eye out for transition phrases like "in addition," "however," or "moreover" – they can lead us to supporting details that might challenge or refine the main ideas. These little linguistic gems open the door to a deeper understanding of the author's thoughts, inviting us to explore the complexities hidden within the text.

Step 6: Master the Art of Summarization

Now that we've successfully navigated the maze of main ideas and supporting details, it's time to put our skills to the test. Summarize the passage in your own words, capturing the essence of the text in a clear and concise statement. This exercise sharpens our ability to synthesize information, grasp the big picture, and communicate effectively. Remember, my friend, practice makes perfect, and with each summary, we're getting closer to mastering this skill.

As we reach the end of our journey through the realms of identifying main ideas and supporting details, let's not forget the value of this skill in our quest for knowledge. With a sharp mind and a discerning eye, we've acquired the tools to unravel the complexity of any text. So, my dear explorer of information, go forth and dive into the intricacies of the written word, for there's a whole world of understanding waiting for your eager mind. May your journey be filled with enlightenment, and may you always treasure the power of recognizing main ideas and supporting details.

2.3 Making Inferences and Drawing Conclusions

I gotta tell ya, folks, here at Test Treasure Publication, we ain't just about readin' some words on a page and callin' it a day. Nah, we're all about diggin' deep, gettin' our hands dirty, and uncoverin' the hidden messages, themes, and ideas that lie beneath the surface. We wanna give students the tools to interact with the material in a profound way, to really get in there and extract meaning that goes beyond what's right in front of 'em.

You see, makin' inferences is all about usin' what we already know, piecin' together the clues, and figurin' out what that author is really tryin' to say. We walk our students through every step of the process, help 'em analyze the details, draw connections, and make educated guesses that bring that text to life.

But that's just the start, my friends. Drawin' conclusions takes it to a whole 'nother level. It's takin' all the info we gathered from the text and makin' sense of it, findin' the patterns, and seein' the big picture. By drawin' those conclusions, we turn all that raw information into somethin' meaningful, somethin' that helps us really understand the text and the world around us.

In this chapter, we're gonna load you up with all kinds of strategies and techniques to beef up your inference and conclusion drawin' skills. Our study guides are packed with explanations that'll make your head spin, examples that'll have you goin' "aha!", and exercises that'll get those brain gears turnin'. We'll show you how to tell the difference between what's implied and what's right there in black and white, how to spot them key details, and how to use all that info you got to come up with some solid conclusions.

But hold on tight, 'cause we're not done yet. We're gonna challenge you to think even deeper, to look beyond the words on the page and see what they're really tryin' to tell us. We believe that readin' ain't just sittin' back and lettin' the words wash over ya. No siree, it's a chance for growth, for discovery. We want you to bring your own experiences, your own knowledge, and your own perspective to the table. That's how we create a learnin' environment that's alive and kickin', that pushes you to really think and engage with that text in a way that means somethin' to you.

So come on down to Test Treasure Publication, where we're all about huntin' down that intellectual treasure. Every text is like a hidden treasure chest just beggin' to be cracked open, and we're here to give you all the tools and guidance you need to find those juicy secrets. Get ready for the thrill of discovery, the satisfaction of unravelin' complex ideas, and the pure joy of divin' into the deep, deep well of knowledge.

Let's do this, folks! Join us at Test Treasure Publication, where we're gonna light that spark of curiosity, fan the flame of intellect, and empower you to unlock all them hidden gems in every single text. Together, we're gonna go on a journey of exploration and enlightenment, where we'll become masters of makin' inferences and drawin' conclusions. Get those shovels ready, 'cause it's gonna be a wild ride!

2.4 Analyzing Tone and Purpose

You know, when it comes to writing, tone is like the secret sauce that adds flavor to the words. It's the author's vibe, their feelings about what they're writing, that really brings the whole thing to life. It's like they're speaking straight to your soul, stirring up all kinds of emotions inside you. Whether they want you to feel sad, happy, mad, or just plain "meh," the tone gives you a glimpse into their perspective and helps you connect with their message on a deeper level.

Now, analyzing tone might sound like some daunting task, but trust me, it's like unlocking a whole new dimension in writing. It's all about paying attention to those little shifts in the author's tone as you read, you know? It's like peeling back the layers of an onion and getting to the juicy core of what they're really trying to say. It's about understanding their emotions and attitudes, and how they want you to feel when you're reading their work. It's like getting a backstage pass to their mind.

But hold up, we can't forget about purpose. Purpose is like the GPS that guides the author's words and shapes their delivery. What are they trying to accomplish with their writing? Are they trying to entertain, inform, convince, or inspire? Knowing the purpose behind a text helps us read with a critical eye, so we can see the strategies that the author is using to achieve their goals. It's like being a detective for literature.

So, when we dive into analyzing tone and purpose, we're really diving into this awesome journey of discovery. We're going deep into the minds of these authors and unearthing the artistry hidden within their words. And luckily, Test Treasure Publication has got your back on this. They've got all these cool study guides, flashcards, and online resources that light the way, so you can navigate the literary landscape like a boss. They understand that you've got your own unique interpretations and perspectives, and they encourage growth and collaboration in their community. Your voice matters to them, and they want to celebrate your insights.

At Test Treasure Publication, they don't just want studying for exams to be some boring process. They want it to be a journey of self-discovery and tapping into your true potential. Their resources go beyond the usual textbooks. They're like mentors that spark your love for learning and guide you towards your goals. They're all about quality, innovation, and, most importantly, your success.

So, let's embrace the challenge of analyzing tone and purpose, my friend, because it's like the key that opens the door to a world of understanding and connection. Join us over at Test Treasure Publication, where the journey of learning is way more than just ordinary. Their study materials become your trusty allies in the pursuit of academic greatness. Let's navigate the intricate terrain of literature together, because within every text, there's a treasure just waiting to be discovered.

2.5 Conclusion

From the moment we started diving into the world of aviation knowledge and breaking down the ins and outs of the SIFT test, we set out on a journey together. It's been a journey of growth, transformation, and expanding our intellectual horizons. I hope this guide has been your guiding light in illuminating the path to your success.

Within the pages of this guide, we've explored the intricate realms of the SIFT exam, unraveling the complexities of each section. We've dissected the Aviation Information section, digging deep into the world of aerodynamics, aviation physiology, and aviation terminology. You've gained a profound understanding of flight principles, the effects of altitude on the body, and the specialized language that fills the air in aviation.

Moving right along, we've tackled the Math Skills section, acquainting you with mathematical concepts like percentages, decimals, and algebra. We've broken down word problems step-by-step so that you not only grasp the math behind it all, but you're also a master at solving problems within tight time constraints.

In the Mechanical Comprehension section, we've dived into the mechanical realm, helping you decipher the inner workings of engines, gears, levers, and more. With detailed explanations and captivating examples, we've aimed to give you a solid grasp of mechanical concepts, equipping you with the skills to analyze mechanical scenarios and apply your knowledge effectively.

The Reading Comprehension section demanded your focus, concentration, and critical thinking abilities. We've explored various reading strategies, emphasized the importance of active reading, and given you practice passages to sharpen your understanding of complex texts. Together, we've mastered the art of deciphering what the author really means, identifying main ideas, and catching subtle textual nuances.

Lastly, the Spatial Apperception section has tested the limits of your spatial reasoning. We've sharpened your visualizing skills, guided you through mental rotations, and even got you thinking in three dimensions. With detailed explanations and exercises, we've aimed to widen your spatial perception, enabling you to conquer this tough section of the SIFT exam.

Now, as we reach the end of this journey through the study guide, I want you to take a moment to reflect on the perseverance and dedication that got you here. You've spent countless hours mastering the material, truly understanding each concept, and fine-tuning your approach to ensure that you triumph on the SIFT exam.

Remember, success isn't just about passing a test; it's a state of mind that flows through your entire being. It's the passion that propels you, the determination that keeps you going, and the belief that greatness is within your reach.

As you face the challenges that lie ahead on your path to aviation greatness, hold onto the knowledge and strategies you've gained from these pages. Let them be your guiding compass as you soar through the unpredictable winds of the SIFT exam and beyond.

Here at Test Treasure Publication, we've always believed in personalized learning and the power of community-driven success. We don't just aim to prepare you for exams; we strive to empower you to embrace a future bursting with unlimited opportunities. We're here to celebrate your achievements, support your dreams, and guide you towards a life enriched by the pursuit of knowledge.

So, my dear reader, as you close this book and embark on your own remarkable journey, remember that every step you take, every challenge you face, and every achievement you unlock brings you one step closer to realizing your dreams. Believe in yourself, trust in your abilities, and let your wings carry you to heights you never thought possible.

Thank you for choosing Test Treasure Publication, where we light the way to extraordinary success. Thank you for allowing us to be a part of your educational journey. May your future be as radiant and limitless as the sky, and may the knowledge you've gained from this study guide propel you towards the triumphs that await you.

Section 3: The Math Skills Test

3.1 Operations: Addition, Subtraction, Multiplication, and Division

Imagine yourself as a conductor, skilled in the art of addition. You bring together numbers of all kinds, creating a beautiful symphony of mathematical harmony. Whether it's adding two simple numbers or tackling the challenge of multiple digits, we've got you covered. With our carefully crafted study materials, you'll gain a deep understanding of place value, regrouping, and even decimal addition.

Now, don't panic when it comes to subtraction. I know it can feel like a battlefield, with numbers hiding their differences. But fear not, my friend! We've armed you with strategies that will turn subtraction into a conquerable mission. Get ready to unravel the mysteries of regrouping, borrowing, and subtracting across different place values. It's time to become the master of numbers!

As we travel deeper into the world of math, we stumble upon multiplication—the art of repeated addition. Picture yourself as an architect, designing intricate patterns of numbers. You'll master the multiplication tables, yes, but that's just the beginning. Explore the beauty of arrays, understand the properties of multiplication, and even learn how to apply it in real-life situations. Let the symphony of multiplication fill your mind as you unlock its incredible potential.

Finally, we arrive at division, where numbers come together to reveal their secrets in the form of fractions and remainders. Here, you'll become a detective, uncovering the hidden factors and divisors that lie within each number. Our study materials will guide you through the process of dividing whole numbers, fractions, and decimals. Prepare to unveil the mysteries of division with precision and confidence.

At Test Treasure Publication, we believe that operations are more than just abstract concepts. They are the building blocks of mathematical literacy and problem-solving skills. Our comprehensive study guides will guide you through the depths of addition, subtraction, multiplication, and division, allowing your mathematical talents to flourish.

Get ready, my dear student, for a journey of transformation. Dive into the world of operations with Test Treasure Publication as your guiding light. We'll light up the path to mathematical excellence, reigniting your passion for learning. With our personalized approach and unwavering commitment to your success, we invite you to join us on this extraordinary expedition towards achievement.

3.2 Positive and Negative Numbers

But hey, before we set off on this wild adventure, let's get our basics straight. In this chapter, we're gonna dig deep into the mysteries of positive and negative numbers so that you can conquer the challenges that lie ahead.

First things first, what even are positive and negative numbers? At the core, positive numbers represent stuff that's more than zero - the good stuff, you know? It's like rays of sunshine on a perfect summer day, bringing all that vibrant energy and endless possibilities into your math world.

On the flip side, negative numbers are like the opposite of positive numbers. They represent stuff that's less than zero - the not-so-happy stuff. They're like the shadows that creep in at twilight, adding a whole lot of depth and complexity to our number game.

Now that we've got the basics down, let's dive headfirst into using positive and negative numbers in those fancy math operations. Get ready for a mind-blowing adventure, packed with insights and techniques that'll make you a math pro and a problem-solving superstar.

Together, we're gonna unlock the magic of adding, subtracting, multiplying, and dividing positive and negative numbers. We'll learn the tricks to adding and subtracting numbers that have the same signs, and we'll unravel the mysteries of subtracting numbers with opposite signs. Then, we'll get all tangled up in the intricacies of multiplying positive and negative numbers, discovering the patterns that make them tick.

But hold on tight, 'cause we're not done yet! We're also gonna uncover the secrets of dividing positive and negative numbers, figuring out how those pesky signs play a role in the final outcome. And trust me, you're gonna face some tough challenges along the way, but with a little determination and newfound knowledge, we'll conquer 'em all.

Get ready to put your thinking cap on, 'cause we'll be diving into a series of mind-bending exercises and mind-melting puzzles that'll level up your problem-solving skills. We'll dive into this whole new world of number lines, where positive and negative numbers get all cozy and harmonious. We'll even throw you into real-life scenarios where you'll need to use your positive and negative number skills to crack some tough nuts and come up with innovative solutions.

As we go deeper into this chapter, the world of positive and negative numbers will come alive right before your eyes. You'll see how it all fits together and how it has a crazy impact on the world around us. So get ready, 'cause we're about to go on a journey that'll equip you with the tools to confidently navigate the twists and turns of positive and negative numbers, opening the doors to endless possibilities and unlocking your true mathematical potential.

So come on, join us on this epic adventure, where Test Treasure Publication lights the way and invites you to step into the thrilling realm of positive and negative numbers - a realm where the beauty of math awaits.

3.3 Factors and Multiples

Let's start by wrapping our heads around the essence of factors. Picture a number, like an entity that's made up of multiple factors. These factors, just like the threads of a tapestry, all come together to create the number, forming something totally unique. So, as we set off on this journey, we'll learn how to spot these factors, plucking them out of the numerical tapestry and really understanding why they matter.

But here's the thing, factors aren't just these random threads - they're all connected, like some complex web of relationships that actually define what these numbers are all about. To really understand this web, we'll dive deep into the world of multiples - these are basically the offspring of factors. Think of them as branches that extend from a tree, reaching out far and wide to show us just how much these factors can influence numbers, no matter how big or how small.

As we go further into the amazing world of factors and multiples, we'll come across this really cool concept of prime numbers - these are like the building blocks of math. They're kind of like these rare gems hidden among all the other numbers, because they have this one amazing trait: they can only be evenly divided by the number one and themselves. They're like these guardians of math, making sure everything stays pure and simple, without any other numbers getting in the way.

But, wait a minute, don't get fooled - prime numbers actually love to dance and play with their counterparts, known as composite numbers. These composite numbers are like all the different elements of a grand symphony, because they have factors beyond just one and themselves. They're these mixtures of numbers that challenge us to find all their different factors and really explore the complicated relationships hidden within them.

On our quest to really understand factors and multiples, we'll unravel the cool world of divisibility rules. These rules are like these guiding constellations in the night sky, showing us how to test if numbers are divisible by other numbers. Like, for example, there's that famous rule that says a number is divisible by 2 if it's even - it's like a shortcut to figuring things out faster! And there are even more rules, like for 3, 5, 7, and so on. It's like we're finding these secret maps, guiding us on a journey to quick and efficient divisibility testing.

And that's not all - as we learn more about factors and multiples, we'll be able to simplify fractions and crack the code of prime factorization. With all this amazing knowledge, we'll be able to untangle all these complex fractions, breaking them down into their simplest forms. And that means we'll be way more ready to solve those tricky math problems with way more ease and accuracy.

So, my friend, get ready to dive into the fascinating world of factors and multiples. Brace yourself for all the mind-blowing wonders waiting just around the corner, 'cause within this realm lies the very foundation upon which all arithmetic and algebra are built. Join us on this epic adventure of discovery, where we'll light up the path to mathematical superpowers and unlock all the incredible knowledge that's hiding within the fascinating world of 8.3 Factors and Multiples.

3.4 Systems of Equations

Welcome to the fascinating world of systems of equations! This is where math becomes a gateway to problem-solving and critical thinking. In this chapter, we'll dive into the intricacies of this topic, unraveling the interconnected relationships between variables and equations. It's like untangling a web of connections, figuring out how everything fits together.

Now, let me break it down for you. A system of equations is a set of equations with one or more variables that are all connected. The challenge is to find the values of those variables that satisfy all the equations at the same time. It's like uncovering a secret code that unlocks a treasure trove of solutions. And trust me, these skills are essential in a wide range of fields, from physics and engineering to economics and computer science.

But hold up! Before we jump into solving these systems, let's talk about the types of solutions we might encounter. We've got three possible scenarios here: a unique solution, infinitely many solutions, or no solution at all. Picture this: a unique solution means that there's only one combination of values that make all the equations happy. On the other hand, infinitely many solutions imply that there are multiple combos that work, like waves crashing on the shore. And finally, no solution means there's no way to make all the equations work together, like oil and water refusing to mix.

Okay, now let's get into the juicy part – how to solve these systems! We'll start with the graphical method. It's like drawing a map that helps us navigate through the maze of equations. We plot the equations on a coordinate plane and find where they intersect. Those points are the magical values that satisfy all the equations at once. But fair warning, this method might not be super accurate when things get complex.

Next up, we've got the substitution method. It's like a game of swap, where we replace one variable with an expression made up of the other variables. By doing this and plugging it into another equation, we can solve for one variable at a time. We keep doing this until we've cracked the code and found all the values. It's like Sherlock Holmes unraveling a mystery, step by step.

Now, here's a real power move – the elimination method. We can also call it the addition/subtraction method. It's like a magic trick where we manipulate the equations to make a variable vanish. We add or subtract equations to make things disappear. By pulling off this trick with precision, we simplify the system and make it easier to solve. It's like tidying up a messy room before a party.

Now that we've got the tools, let's see where we can apply this mathematical wizardry in the real world. Take economics, for example. Systems of equations can help us model supply and demand, figuring out the perfect balance in the market. In physics, they describe the relationships between variables, helping us predict and understand the wild phenomena of the universe. And guess what? You can even use systems of equations in everyday life, like finding the perfect recipe proportions or budgeting wisely.

But remember, practice makes perfect! As you work through this chapter, we'll give you plenty of examples and exercises to sharpen your skills. Approach each problem methodically, choosing the right technique and taking it step by step. Celebrate every victory, big or small, as a testament to your growing expertise. And if you need help, don't hesitate to reach out for guidance.

So, dear student, immerse yourself in the world of systems of equations. Embrace the challenges, for in your hands lies the treasure of knowledge and the key to extraordinary success. Let's go on this journey together and unlock the power of math!

3.5 Polynomial Algebra

Have you ever stopped to think about how powerful polynomial algebra can be? It's like this magical branch of math that helps us understand the relationships between numbers and variables. It's all about these expressions with variables, coefficients, and exponents that come together to create these mind-boggling equations. And let me tell you, these equations, they have a beauty and elegance to them that is just awe-inspiring.

But the best part is how polynomial algebra can actually help us solve real-world problems. It's like this secret weapon we have in our math arsenal. You see, we're gonna dive deep into the art of simplifying polynomial expressions. We'll untangle all these complex webs of terms and coefficients and really get to the heart of what makes them tick. It's like pulling back the curtain and revealing the hidden symmetry and order that lies within.

But solving equations is where polynomial algebra really shines. We're gonna tackle equations of all different degrees - from simple linear ones to those funky quadratic ones and even crazier higher-order polynomials. And trust me, each step is gonna be like unraveling a mystery. We'll use these cool techniques like factoring and synthetic division to crack the code and find the solutions.

And get this, we're even gonna learn how to divide polynomials, just like how we divide numbers. It's this thing called polynomial long division, and it's gonna blow your mind. We're gonna strip away all the complicated layers of these polynomial expressions and simplify them down to their most elegant forms. It's like solving a puzzle and finding the perfect solution.

But wait, there's more! We're gonna dive into the significance of zeros and factors too. These are like the keys to unlocking the behavior of polynomials. They help us find the roots and graph these crazy curves. It's like we're becoming detectives, searching for clues and unraveling the mysteries of these polynomial equations on the good ol' Cartesian coordinate system.

Oh, and polynomial functions? They're a whole other ballgame. They take these algebraic expressions and bring them to life on graphs and curves. We're gonna analyze their behavior, find their zeros and intercepts, and see how they transform and twist. It's like watching a symphony play out right in front of our eyes.

This journey through the world of polynomial algebra is gonna be one heck of a ride. It's filled with patterns and symmetries that'll leave you in awe. It's like this dance of numbers and symbols that you never knew existed. So come on, let's dive in together. Let's marvel at the beauty of this field, and let's unlock the secrets of the mathematical universe. Are you with me? Let's embark on this quest for knowledge, enlightenment, and unbelievable success.

3.6 Solving Quadratic Equations

Alright, folks, get ready to dive into the fascinating world of quadratic equations. These bad boys have some serious power, so it's crucial to wrap our heads around them before we start solving them.

A quadratic equation is a fancy term for a polynomial equation of degree two. Basically, it's an equation that equals zero and has three main components: the coefficient of the quadratic term (let's call it "a"), the coefficient of the linear term ("b"), and the constant term ("c"). We usually write it like this: $ax^2 + bx + c = 0$.

Now, buckle up because we're about to explore the properties and behavior of quadratic equations. These are the fundamental concepts that will guide us on our quest to solve them. We'll unravel the mysteries of the discriminant, the vertex form, and completing the square technique. Trust me, these insights will give you the tools you need to conquer any quadratic equation that comes your way.

Step 2: It's time to unleash the power of the quadratic formula. This baby's like a treasure map that leads us straight to the roots of any quadratic equation. The formula comes from this fancy technique called completing the square. Long story short, it transforms the equation into a solvable form. So, the solution to a quadratic equation $ax^2 + bx + c = 0$ is given by $x = (-b \pm \sqrt{b^2 - 4ac})/2a$. Pretty wild, right? Oh, and don't forget to check the discriminant, that little guy inside the square root. It determines whether the equation has real or complex roots. $\Delta = b^2 - 4ac$ will spill the beans!

Armed with this formula, you'll be unstoppable when it comes to solving those mind-boggling quadratic equations. You'll uncover their secrets and bask in the glory of your triumphs. Talk about being the math hero!

Step 3: Now, let's talk factoring techniques. While quadratic formula is like your trusty sidekick, it's not always the fastest way to crack the code. That's when factoring becomes your superhero power. By breaking down the equation into its factors, you can find the roots. It's all about spotting common factors or using tricks like grouping, difference of squares, or perfect square trinomials. Once you've got those techniques down, there's no quadratic equation you can't handle!

Step 4: Practice, practice, practice. Like anything in life, practice is the key to becoming a master. That's why we've got a ton of exercises and problems lined up for you. These puppies are designed to challenge you and refine your skills in quadratic equation solving. But remember, it's not just about finding the answers. It's about understanding the principles and concepts behind each solution. That deep understanding will give you the confidence to tackle any quadratic equation that crosses your path. You'll be a mathematical legend!

Closing Note: Congrats, my dear student, for embarking on this enlightening journey into the world of quadratic equations. With the wisdom you've gained from reading these pages, you're ready to conquer even the trickiest math enigmas. And hey, Test Treasure Publication is more than just study materials. We're here to be your academic companion on this wild ride. We believe in your ability to reach incredible heights, and we're here to guide and empower you every step of the way.

So, my fellow learners, let's venture forth together, united by our passion for learning, and unlock the hidden treasures of the quadratic equation realm. Are you ready? Let's do this!

3.7 Basic Geometry

Imagine a time before textbooks and study guides, when the ancient Egyptians labored meticulously to construct massive pyramids that matched the patterns of the celestial bodies above. These were the architects of geometric principles, shaping the foundations that would later be expanded upon by the insatiable thirst for knowledge of the Greeks. They delivered mathematical marvels that paved the way for the geometry we know today.

But let's not get lost in the ancient past. We're about to embark on a journey through the vast expanse of geometry. And trust me, it's essential to understand the fundamental building blocks that shape this mysterious discipline. It all starts with points - little infinitesimal specks that hold within them the potential for endless creations. It's like a microscopic universe waiting to burst into existence.

But don't think the points are lonely. They're connected to one another by lines, creating a framework that builds the geometric world before your eyes. These lines are like threads weaving a beautiful tapestry - straight lines that stretch infinitely in opposing directions, or curved lines gracefully tracing the contours of space. It's like watching a painter meticulously putting brushstrokes onto a canvas, revealing the elegance hidden within these infinite pathways.

Now, here's where the plot thickens: angles. They're these intricate intersections of lines that hold some serious power. They can transform our perception of space, making us see things in a whole new light. In this chapter, we're tearing the veil off the hidden secrets of angles, unveiling their properties and relationships. We dive into the realm of acute angles, sharp and precise, guiding us through the complexities of geometry. Then there are those obtuse angles, so open and expansive, reminding us of all the possibilities that exist beyond the boundaries we've set for ourselves. And we can't ignore the ever-elusive right angle - a symbol of harmony and balance, cornerstoning the way we understand geometric structures.

Hold on, because it's about to get even more interesting. As we venture deeper into basic geometry, we encounter shapes - the celestial bodies of this geometric universe. Triangles take the stage, with their three sides and three angles, holding the key to unlocking the mysteries of proportion and congruence. Then there are squares, rectangles, and parallelograms - balanced sides and equal angles that mesmerize us with their symmetrical beauty. And let's not forget the captivating circles, with their infinite curves and perfect symmetry. They ignite our imaginations and captivate our eyes like no other.

Are you ready for this chapter? Buckle up, because we're going to equip you with the tools to navigate these geometrical wonders. We won't let shapes be confined to mere drawings on a page. Instead, we'll bring them to life in your mind, giving them dimensions and characteristics that breathe life into the abstract.

Dear reader, prepare yourself for an odyssey through the geometric realm. We're about to transcend boundaries, uncover hidden truths, and witness the beauty of mathematical perfection embodied in shapes. Together, we'll unlock the secrets of geometry and discover the treasures that lie within its depths. So, join me on this extraordinary journey, where Test Treasure Publication will become not just your guide but your companion in unraveling the enchanting world of basic geometry.

3.8 Conclusion

Hey there! Can I just say, this journey we've been on together has been something else, huh? From the very beginning, Test Treasure Publication has been right there, working hard to make sure you succeed. And boy, have we cooked up something special for you. This study guide we've put together isn't your average one, oh no. It's a game-changer. It's gonna take you to heights you never even dreamed of.

But listen, this journey isn't just about facts and figures or acing exams. It's about discovering who you really are. It's about diving deep into critical thinking, problem-solving, and having a mind that can tackle anything thrown your way. Think of this as an invitation to become not just any old test-taker, but a true scholar who can make their way through the twists and turns of their chosen field with total clarity and confidence.

You know, this book isn't just a collection of information. It's like having a mentor right there with you, guiding you and helping you find that drive to learn and be your absolute best. We've got your back, my friend.

Now, as we come to the end of this study guide, I want you to take a moment to reflect on how far you've come. Remember when you first picked up this book? You were so unsure and nervous. But now, look at you. You've grown so much, and that confidence is shining through. You're ready to conquer your exams, and even more than that, you're equipped to tackle any challenge that comes your way.

But hey, don't think our commitment ends here. The Test Treasure Publication community is here to support you long after you close this book. We've set up all kinds of online resources, forums, and communities so you can keep growing, stay curious, and connect with others who are on the same journey as you.

And here's the thing, success isn't just about test scores or accomplishments. It's about a deep dedication to personal growth, it's about always learning, and it's about striving for excellence in everything you do. So as you take the next steps on your academic journey, hold onto the lessons you've learned from these pages. They're like a guiding light, showing you the way to extraordinary success.

Thank you again for choosing Test Treasure Publication as your partner on this incredible voyage. As you close this book, remember that we're still on this journey together. We're gonna rise above the norm and grab every single opportunity that comes our way. With Test Treasure Publication on your side, there's no limit to what you can achieve. Your future is so bright, my friend.

Now, my dear reader, go out there and embrace your potential. Let your brilliance shine. May greatness follow you in everything you do, knowing that success isn't just a finish line, but a lifelong adventure. So for now, farewell. But don't worry, our paths will cross again. Take care, my friend.

Section 4: The Mechanical Comprehension Test

4.1 Kinetics

Hey there! Imagine yourself standing at the edge of something truly incredible. The air is buzzing with excitement as molecules collide, dance, and transform, shaping our universe as we know it. It's in this magical realm that we dive into the study of kinetics, where we unravel the mysteries of how reactions happen.

Now, our journey kicks off by exploring the heartbeat of chemical transformations: reaction rates. We'll dig into the factors that influence the speed at which reactions occur, like temperature, concentration, and the presence of catalysts. Think of it like finding the perfect balance between ingredients and how fast they turn into something totally new.

But hold on to your seat, because it gets even more fascinating! We're going to peek behind the curtains of the chemical stage production. Imagine yourself as a spectator, witnessing molecules take on roles and creating a tale of molecular encounters and intricate steps. You'll see molecules collide, forming activated complexes, and ultimately becoming something completely different. It's like watching a movie unfold right before your eyes!

And that's not all! Get ready to crunch some numbers as we dive into reaction orders and rate laws. We'll uncover the math that governs the speed of these reactions, revealing the hidden secrets within those chemical formulas. It's like unlocking a whole new world of understanding how different chemical systems behave.

To make sure you really grasp the concept, we'll get interactive! We'll do exercises and ponder over thought-provoking questions that relate kinetics to real-world scenarios. By getting hands-on, you'll develop an intuition that'll help you predict reactions and make smart choices in complex chemical situations.

But wait, there's more! As our journey nears its end, we'll zoom out and reflect on how kinetics influences the world around us. It's not just about understanding reactions; it's about the impact it has on designing efficient industrial processes and developing life-saving drugs. By mastering kinetics, you're wielding the power to shape the world and drive innovation forward.

So, get ready for this mind-blowing expedition through the world of kinetics. Let this chapter be your doorway into a realm where molecules collide, reactions happen, and the secrets of chemical transformations are unveiled. And always remember, knowledge is not just a treasure, it's the catalyst for extraordinary success.

Welcome to the enchanting world of kinetics—where science dances with discovery.

4.2 Work/Energy

When it comes to the fascinating world of physics, work and energy are like two best friends who always stick together. They create this beautiful symphony of knowledge that tickles our curious minds and urges us to explore. Work is all about transfer of energy, y'know? It happens when a force acts on an object and makes it move in the same direction as the force. But it's not just about physical labor, there's a whole universe of mechanics behind it.

This whole interplay between work and energy is what helps us understand how things in motion behave. From the graceful flight of a bird in the sky to the powerful waves crashing onto the shore, work and energy are the backbone of nature itself. It's like they've got a backstage pass to all the cool stuff happening around us.

But there's more to the story. The conservation of energy is like the icing on the cake. In this world, energy can't be created or destroyed. It just transforms from one form to another. Picture it as this captivating dance where energy gets converted and preserved. From an object's potential energy, which is stored up because of its position, to its kinetic energy, which is all about that energy in motion. It's like watching a symphony of energy that explains all the amazing things we see around us every day.

If we look at work and energy through a different lens, we start to see the relationship between force and distance. See, when forces act on objects and push them a certain distance, we can measure the amount of work done using a simple equation. It's like Fd, where W is work, F is force, and d is the distance over which the force is applied. When we unravel this equation, we get insights into all the mighty forces shaping our world.

But it's not just about crunching numbers and doing math, my friend. The study of work and energy takes us on a philosophical journey, exploring the very essence of our existence. It invites us to ponder the interconnectedness of forces and energies, not just in the physical world but within ourselves as well. It's like blowing our own minds when we realize the potential we all have.

Deep within the study of work and energy, there's a truth that hits us like a lightning bolt. We each have this wellspring of energy inside us, eagerly waiting to be unleashed and put to good use. By understanding the mechanics of work and energy, we unlock the door to our own potential. We transform dreams into reality and passions into purpose.

So, my dear reader, as we set sail on this captivating journey into the land of work and energy, let's not just think of it as another subject to study. Let's see it as a gateway to discovering ourselves. Let's dive into the complexities, savoring every moment of revelation and awakening. In the pages of this study guide, we'll unravel the mysteries of the universe and ignite that inner spark that drives us to be great.

Welcome to this enchanting world of work and energy where the possibilities are endless and incredible accomplishments await us. Together, let's embark on this profound journey, as we uncover the power that lies within each and every one of us.

4.3 Machines

Machines, my friend, are like the physical embodiment of our brilliant minds. I mean, think about it - from a simple lever to a super fancy computer, they have seriously shaped our world. I'm talking about major feats accomplished, challenges conquered, and even harnessing the raw power of nature!

Now, in this chapter, we're gonna dive deep into the inner workings of machines and discover the secret sauce that makes them tick. We'll get all up in their mechanisms, whether it's the energy conversion game or that fancy force amplification stuff. And boy, oh boy, we're gonna explore all types of machines - the basic dudes like pulleys and inclined planes, and the more complex folks like engines and turbines.

But hold on a sec, machines are more than just a bunch of gears and bolts. They're the real unsung heroes, my friend. Think back to the industrial revolution - those bad boys totally transformed industry and brought in some mega innovation.

Like, for real, the steam engine was a magical wonder that powered transportation and manufacturing like nobody's business.

So, as we go on this wild ride through the land of machines, get ready to be blown away by all these gears, levers, and pulleys. We're gonna unravel the mysteries of mechanical advantage and efficiency, and maybe even touch on the almighty principles of motion.

I gotta say, machines are seriously mind-blowing. From a tiny little watch to a freaking space shuttle, they're always pushing the boundaries of what's possible. They're sorta like the rockstars of progress - super precise and incredibly powerful. It's because of machines that we can unleash the hidden forces of the universe and bring our wildest dreams to life.

So, my friend, let's go on this captivating journey together. We'll dig deep into the world of machines, and really get a feel for how they've woven themselves into the very fabric of our society. We'll understand their inner workings and appreciate the sheer artistry that goes into their creation. You see, studying machines is more than just learning some random stuff. It's like unraveling this magnificent tapestry of human ingenuity.

4.4 Momentum/Impulse

Ah, momentum and impulse – two fascinating concepts in physics that have captured my attention in the SIFT Study Guide. We're about to venture into the mesmerizing world of motion and collisions, where we'll discover how these fundamental principles shape the behavior of objects in motion.

Let's start with momentum. It's this magical combination of an object's mass and its velocity, and it serves as a measure of the motion's persistence. It's like that inherent "oomph" an object possesses, resisting any changes in its state of motion. Pretty cool, huh? And as we dive deeper into this concept, we'll uncover its intricate connection to impulse.

Now, impulse is all about the change in momentum that an external force imparts on an object. Picture this force acting on the object for a certain duration of time, causing either an increase or decrease in momentum. It's like this dance between forces and objects, especially during collisions – where the forces really make a difference in altering their movements.

In the world of physics, momentum and impulse control all sorts of mind-blowing phenomena. Imagine the breathtaking spectacle of a speeding bullet impacting its target or the elegant ballet of billiard balls colliding on a table. These concepts unlock the secrets of the universe's grand dance of motion, and we're privileged to dive into their intricacies.

Now, let me break down the topics we'll cover in this section, which are bound to blow your mind:

1. Conservation of Momentum: We're about to explore one of the most profound laws in physics – the conservation of momentum. This concept allows us to predict and understand the outcomes of collisions and why some defy logic. It's like unraveling the hidden mysteries of motion.

2. Impulse-Momentum Principle: Brace yourself for the impulse-momentum principle, a powerful tool that connects the change in momentum to the force exerted on an object. Through mind-boggling examples and problem-solving exercises, we'll see how force, time, and momentum are all beautifully linked.

3. Elastic and Inelastic Collisions: Here's where things get really interesting. We'll dive into the different types of collisions that objects can undergo – elastic and inelastic collisions. By understanding the unique properties of each type, we'll

gain insights into real-world scenarios, like car accidents, where the preservation or loss of kinetic energy becomes crucial.

4. Explosion Problems: Let's venture into the exciting world of explosions – where objects initially at rest suddenly separate with tremendous velocities. Buckle up as we analyze momentum and impulse to unravel the principles behind these explosive phenomena. It's like watching fireworks of knowledge in action!

5. Recoil Problems: Last but not least, we'll explore recoil problems, where the propulsion of an object creates backward motion in another. It's a bit mind-bending, but we'll unravel how the momenta and masses of these interacting bodies intertwine to create these unexpected consequences. Get ready for surprises, my friend!

Throughout this section, get ready for a thrilling journey. We're about to dive deep into the realms of momentum and impulse, arming ourselves with the skills and insights necessary to tackle the challenges these concepts present. So, gear up, my friend, because understanding momentum and impulse will reveal the true secrets of the universe's incessant dance of motion. Let's do this!

4.5 Fluids

Hey there! Have you ever stopped to think about just how important studying fluids really is? I mean, seriously, take a moment to imagine a river gracefully winding through a peaceful landscape or the way a summer breeze gently rustles through those towering trees. It's all connected, you know? Fluid dynamics is everywhere, shaping the very fabric of our existence.

These fluids, they have this unique charm to them. With their special properties, they follow these rules of pressure, volume, and temperature that just show us how perfectly balanced the natural world really is. And you know what? Understanding these rules opens up a whole bunch of possibilities. We can predict and explain so many things by diving into the amazing realm of fluid dynamics.

So get ready, my friend, because we're about to embark on a journey like no other. A journey that unravels the secrets of fluid motion and the forces that shape our entire universe. We're going in deep, exploring the complex world of fluid mechanics, to uncover the principles that govern how liquids and gases behave. And let me tell you, it's a wild ride, but totally worth it.

In this chapter, we're diving headfirst into the fundamental concepts of fluid dynamics. We'll break down the principles of pressure and buoyancy and really get into the nitty-gritty of fluid flow. We're gonna analyze factors that influence velocity, viscosity, and turbulence, because understanding these things helps us make sense of real-life applications. We'll be talking about everything from how blood circulates in our bodies to the aerodynamics of airplanes soaring through the skies. Pretty cool, right?

Now, I gotta warn you, there will be math involved. We're gonna dig into the equations of fluid mechanics, because hey, that's how we solve problems. But trust me, there's more to it than just numbers and formulas. There's this whole other level of understanding waiting for us. It's like peeling back the layers and realizing that beneath the ordinary stuff we see every day, there's this hidden world controlled by the laws of fluid mechanics.

So as we venture through this chapter, I want us to remember that this journey we're on isn't just about the end result. It's about personal growth, discovery, and that feeling of awe. Studying fluids gives us a chance to unlock the mysteries of the world, to catch a glimpse of the underlying order that hides behind the seeming chaos around us.

So let's immerse ourselves in the wonder of fluids, my friend. Let's strive for a comprehensive understanding of how they behave. With our dedication and perseverance, we'll unlock the limitless potential held within the fluid realm. This realm goes way beyond the boundaries of this study guide, encapsulating the wonders of the natural world. So let's go, together, fueled by our shared curiosity, unwavering determination, and our hunger for knowledge. Welcome to the chapter on fluids—a place where beauty and complexity come together, turning the ordinary into something extraordinary.

4.6 Heat Transfer

In this chapter, we're gonna dive deep into the fascinating world of heat transfer. We're gonna explore all the nitty-gritty details of how heat moves from one thing to another. And trust me, it's gonna blow your mind! We're gonna go on a quest to unravel the mysteries of this powerful force and how we can use it in practical ways.

So, let's start with conduction. Picture this, you're sitting at a table, and there's a steaming bowl of soup in front of you. You grab a metal spoon, dip it into the soup, and boom! The spoon starts getting warmer. This is all a result of conduction, my friend. The heat from the soup is traveling through direct contact with the spoon's molecules. It's like a secret language whispered between them. Understanding this concept is key in so many scientific and engineering fields. It's mind-blowing!

Next up, we've got convection. Imagine yourself gathered around a toasty campfire on a chilly evening. The flames are dancing and crackling, and the air around you is getting all cozy. Here's the thing - heat is being transferred through the movement of the air! The warm air rises, creating this beautiful dance, while colder air swoops in to take its place. It's like a hot and cold tango. Convection is everywhere, from our atmosphere to fans and pumps. It affects weather, air circulation, and even how our gadgets stay cool. It's mind-boggling, really.

Lastly, we've got radiation. It's like this cool magical thing, man! Picture a sunny day, and you feel that sweet warmth on your skin. That's radiation, my friend. It doesn't need any physical medium, it just travels through electromagnetic waves. It's like the sun giving you a warm embrace or a red-hot piece of coal radiating heat. Radiation plays a huge role in astrophysics, solar energy, and building design. It's like a cosmic dance of warmth.

By delving into these different modes of heat transfer, we're gonna open up a whole new world of understanding. We'll see how they all work together in the real world and how we can apply this knowledge in practical ways. We're talking about designing insulation that's super efficient, creating advanced cooling systems for our precious electronics, and even figuring out how to manage heat in space vehicles. It's gonna be epic.

So, come on this journey with me, my friend! Let's venture into the enchanting realm of heat transfer. We'll unlock its secrets, unravel its principles, and light a fire of passion for the science behind all the warmth that surrounds us. Let's get ready to rock the world of heat transfer and take our academic pursuits to the next level. It's gonna be extraordinary, I promise you that.

4.7 Optics

Welcome to the captivating world of optics, where the flick of a switch reveals mind-blowing landscapes governed by the laws of physics and illuminated by the mesmerizing dance of light. It's like stepping into another realm, one where we explore the secrets of light waves, their characteristics, and how they change their paths as they encounter different stuff.

Let's start our journey with reflection, an enigmatic process that alters the path of light when it bumps into something reflective. It's fascinating how this phenomenon mirrors the reflections we encounter in our own lives, don't you think?

It's like the world of optics has a story to tell, one that's relatable and beautifully complex. And as we dive deeper into this magical realm, we'll uncover the laws that govern reflection and get lost in a world of ray diagrams and the principles of image formation.

But we won't stop there. Oh no, my friend, we're going to venture further into the unknown and explore the phenomenon of refraction. Prepare to have your preconceived notions challenged and your understanding of light shattered as we witness the bending of light waves when they pass through different mediums. It's like they have a mind of their own, changing direction while still keeping us captivated by their essence. And you know what? We're going to understand it all by delving into Snell's law and the concept of critical angles. Just imagine the gateway to comprehension swinging wide open!

And then there's diffraction, the bending and spreading of light waves as they encounter tiny obstacles or squeeze through tight openings. This is where things get really interesting. The size of the obstacle or opening dictates the degree of diffraction, creating a mesmerizing dance that challenges our imagination. It's like the universe is teasing us with its vastness, reminding us of the endless potential hiding within its wonders.

So, come on this wondrous journey with us as we navigate the intricate world of optics. Our trusty study guide will be your companion, unraveling the complexities and shedding light on the path to profound understanding. Prepare to be amazed with detailed explanations, captivating illustrations, and thought-provoking exercises that empower you to transcend the ordinary and embrace the extraordinary.

Together, let's embark on this enlightening expedition through the realm of optics, where every page unravels a new layer of knowledge and inspiration. We'll navigate the complexities of reflection, refraction, and diffraction, unlocking the secrets of light and harnessing its magnificent power. With Test Treasure Publication as your guide, get ready to dive into the depths of optics, where the brilliance of science collides with the wonders of the universe to shape your success and propel you to remarkable achievements.

4.8 Electricity

Alright, folks, let's dive into the wild world of electric circuits! Picture this: a complex maze of interconnected pathways, like some kind of electric wonderland, guiding the flow of tiny electrons through a conductor. We're gonna crack the code of resistors, capacitors, and inductors, unraveling their secrets and understanding how they mess with the flow of electric current. Once we've mastered the art of circuit analysis, we'll be like circuit detectives, breezing through even the trickiest networks, reading the language of electricity like it's no big deal.

But wait, there's more! As we journey deeper into the electric realm, things get even more mysterious and mind-blowing. Get ready for the phenomenon of electromagnetic fields, where invisible forces collide and charged particles do a cosmic dance. We're gonna uncover the thrilling connection between electric and magnetic fields, and how they mess with each other's business. Maxwell's equations are gonna be our tour guides, showing us the juicy relationships between electric and magnetic fields, the whole shebang. Brace yourselves, because reality as you know it is about to get a serious makeover. You won't be seeing electricity the same way again.

So, what's at the heart of this whole electricity gig, you wonder? Well, grab a front-row seat and let's tear apart the fundamental concepts that underpin this electrifying world. We're gonna break down the principles of voltage, current, and resistance, peering into the mesmerizing dance of electrons shimmying through conductors. Ohm's Law is gonna be our best buddy, showing us how voltage, current, and resistance are all tangled up in this perfectly balanced performance.

And don't even get me started on series and parallel circuits, where the elegance of electrical engineering truly shines.

But our journey doesn't end with understanding how electricity works, folks. We gotta be smart about harnessing its power, keeping ourselves safe and sound. In this chapter, we're exploring the nitty-gritty of electrical safety. It's all about avoiding the danger lurking in dodgy wiring and improper use of electrical gadgets. Get ready to become an ambassador for electrical safety as we delve into grounding, circuit protection devices, and the importance of insulation. Safety first, my friends.

As we near the end of our epic adventure through the realm of electricity, take a moment to let it all sink in. From the humble light bulb brightening our lives to the intricate circuits fueling our gadgets, electricity is the backbone of our modern world. Armed with the knowledge gained on this journey, you'll be primed to unveil the mysteries of electricity, tap into its power, and shape the future with your newfound wisdom. But hold your horses, we're not done just yet! Next up, we're diving headfirst into the captivating universe of magnetism and its crazy connection to electricity. Get ready to witness the enchanting dance of magnetic fields and unravel the deep relationship between magnetism and electric current. Trust me, it's gonna be one exhilarating ride. So buckle up and join me as we uncover the secrets that lie within the magnetic realm. Get ready to have your mind blown, my friends.

4.9 Magnetism

Hey there! Get ready for an awesome experience as we dive into chapter 9.9: Magnetism on this incredible journey through the world of science. Trust me, you're in for a wild ride as we explore the mysterious and enchanting realm of magnetic forces - where attraction and repulsion do this intricate dance.

In this chapter, we're going to unravel the mind-blowing secrets behind how magnetism actually works. We'll be exploring the laws, principles, and concepts that govern this captivating force. Believe me, this is where the magic happens - we'll be uncovering the mysteries of magnetic fields, inducing electromotive force, and discovering the wonders of magnetic materials. Can you feel the excitement building up?

Step 1: Get ready for the mind-blowing world of magnetic fields. Picture this - a magical invisible force field that surrounds a magnet, drawing objects towards it or pushing them away. It's like something out of a sci-fi film! These magnetic fields shape our understanding of the world around us, and we're going on a visual journey through these intricate lines and patterns. Brace yourself, because we're about to witness the captivating interaction between these fields and external objects. It's a whole new dimension, my friend!

Step 2: Now, let's turn our attention to magnetic materials. Ever wonder why some materials are magnetic while others remain completely unfazed by magnetic forces? We're about to unravel that mystery! Prepare to be immersed in a fascinating world of ferromagnetic, paramagnetic, and diamagnetic materials. Each material has its own unique characteristics - from retaining magnetism after being magnetized to only being attracted temporarily to magnetic fields or even downright resisting them. It's like they have a mind of their own! We'll be uncovering the hidden secrets that lie within the atomic makeup of these materials – prepare to be amazed!

Step 3: Brace yourself for an electrifying adventure! When magnetic fields and electrical currents come together, something extraordinary happens - electromotive force is generated. We're diving into the captivating world of electrical induction and magnetic flux. We'll explore Faraday's law of electromagnetic induction, analyzing the factors that influence the magnitude of this incredible force. From electric generators to transformers, we'll reveal the practical applications of electromotive force in our daily lives. Get ready to have your mind blown by the mind-bending world of inductions and magnetic interactions!

Step 4: Alright, now let's see how magnetism shapes our world in practical ways. From something as simple as a refrigerator magnet to the mind-boggling technology of MRI machines, magnetism is everywhere! Get ready to be awestruck as we delve into the workings of electric motors and magnetic levitation. We'll even explore how magnetism plays a vital role in telecommunications - guiding information through tiny circuits. You won't believe how magnets are transforming transportation and defying gravity! It's like living in a sci-fi movie, I tell you!

Step 5: Now, it's time to become a magnetism virtuoso! We're going to consolidate your knowledge and make sure you have a deep understanding of this awe-inspiring force. Through practice questions, interactive exercises, and insightful explanations, we're going to solidify your grasp on the intricacies of magnetism. We believe in unlocking your full potential and attracting success in your academic pursuits. With our tailored study materials, you'll become a magnetism master in no time!

So, get ready to be mesmerized by the beauty of magnetism. It's not just a fickle force, but a captivating dance between attraction and repulsion. Together, let's unlock the secrets of magnetic forces and transcend ordinary learning into extraordinary achievement. Join us at Test Treasure Publication, where we unveil the wonders of magnetism and help you excel in your academic journey. It's going to be incredible!

4.10 Conclusion

You know, when we take a step back and compare things, it's like we've stumbled upon this cool little magic trick. It's like connecting the dots and watching something amazing unfold right before our eyes. We find these shared traits and similarities, and it's like we're navigating through this crazy maze of knowledge, building this solid foundation for deeper understanding to grow.

But you know what's just as enchanting? Contrast. It's like putting two completely different things next to each other and seeing all these hidden nuances and complexities emerge. It's celebrating the differences and individuality that make each thing, each person, unique. And let me tell you, when we celebrate that diversity, it's like we're creating this beautiful mosaic of perspectives and experiences that reflect the true depth of what it means to be human.

And here's the kicker - comparison and contrast, they go hand in hand. They dance together, these seemingly opposing forces of similarity and difference. Through this dance, we become these critical thinkers who can navigate the complexities of the world with grace. It's like we've mastered the art of discernment, all because we've learned how to compare and contrast.

We've explored so many different ways to use these skills, too. Think about it - from analyzing literature to diving into scientific research, comparison and contrast take our understanding to a whole new level. We dissect texts, finding hidden meanings that go beyond the surface. We dig into scientific phenomena, connecting the dots and figuring out how things are related. It's like we're these smart observers, always seeking out the truth.

So here we are, at the end of this chapter. Let's take a moment to reflect on just how transformative comparison and contrast can be. Let's appreciate the beauty in both unity and diversity, because they both matter and make our human experience richer. And let's not forget to keep embracing the art of discernment, because it's through comparing and contrasting that we uncover the universe's secrets.

As we turn the page and move forward in our learning journey, let's take the wisdom we've gained from all this comparison and contrast with us. Let's celebrate the connections that bring us together and the differences that make us grow. And let's always remember that the real treasure isn't in the answers we find, but in the questions we dare to ask.

5.1 FULL-LENGTH PRACTICE TEST 1

Section 1: The Army Aviation Information Test

1. Topic: Aerodynamics

Question 1: Which of the following factors does not affect the lift of an aircraft?

A) Airspeed

B) Altitude

C) Color

D) Air Density

2. Topic: Flight Controls

Question 2: Which control surface is primarily used to control roll?

A) Ailerons

B) Rudder

C) Elevators

D) Flaps

3. Topic: Weight and Balance

Question 3: What is the consequence of an aircraft being tail-heavy?

A) Increased Lift

B) Reduced Speed

C) Instability

D) Reduced Drag

4. Topic: Basic Maneuvers

Question 4: During a climb, what generally happens to the airspeed?

A) Increases

B) Decreases

C) Remains Constant

D) Becomes Zero

Section 2: The Reading Comprehension Test

5. Topic: Strategies

Question 5: What is the most effective strategy for tackling inference-based questions?

A) Skimming the passage

B) Reading the questions first

C) Guessing

D) Close reading of the passage

6. Topic: General Reading Comprehension Skills

Question 6: The main idea of a passage is usually found in which part?

A) Beginning

B) Middle

C) End

D) Anywhere in the passage

Section 3: The Math Skills Test

7. Topic: Operations

Question 7: What is the result of 5+3×2?

A) 11

B) 16

C) 13

D) 21

80

8. Topic: Positive and Negative Numbers

Question 8: Which of the following is true?

A) $-3 > -2$

B) $-3 < -2$

C) $-3 = -2$

D) $-3 < 2$

9. Topic: Factors and Multiples

Question 9: Which of the following is a factor of 36?

A) 8

B) 10

C) 4

D) 12

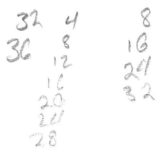

10. Topic: Systems of Equations

Question 10: What is the solution to the system of equations $x+y=5$ and $x-y=1$?

A) $x=2, y=3$

B) $x=3, y=2$

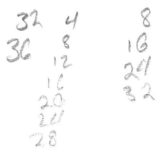

C) $x=4, y=1$

D) $x=1, y=4$

11. Topic: Polynomial Algebra

Question 11: What is the simplified form of $(x+2)^2$?

A) x^2+4x+4

$x^2 + 4$

B) x^2+4

C) x^2+2x+2

D) $2x^2+4$

12. Topic: Solving Quadratic Equations

Question 12: What are the roots of $x^2-3x+2=0$?

A) 1,2

B) $-1,-2$

C) 2,-1

D) 1,-2

$$\frac{2}{-1 \times -2}$$
$$-3$$

$$(x-1)(x-2)$$
$$x-1=0 \quad x-2=0$$
$$x=1 \quad x=2$$

13. Topic: Bas

Question 13: What is the sum of interior angles of a triangle?

A) 90 degrees

B) 180 degrees

C) 360 degrees

D) 270 degrees

Section 4: The Mechanical Comprehension Test

14. Topic: Kinetics

Question 14: What is the formula for kinetic energy?

A) $KE=1/2\ mv^2$

B) $KE=mv$

C) $KE=mgh$

D) $KE=ma$

15. Topic: Work/Energy

Question 15: What is the unit of work?

A) Newton-meter (Nm)

B) Joule (J)

C) Watt (W)

D) Ampere (A)

16. Topic: Machines

Question 16: What is the mechanical advantage of a lever with an effort arm of 4m and a load arm of 2m?

A) 0.5

B) 1

C) 2

D) 4

17. Topic: Momentum/Impulse

Question 17: What is the momentum of an object with a mass of 5 kg moving at a speed of 3 m/s?

A) 5 Ns

B) 8 Ns

C) 15 Ns

D) 20 Ns

18. Topic: Fluids

Question 18: Which principle explains why a boat floats?

A) Bernoulli's Principle

B) Archimedes' Principle

C) Newton's Third Law

D) Pascal's Law

19. Topic: Heat Transfer

Question 19: Which mode of heat transfer is primarily responsible for heating the Earth's surface?

A) Conduction

B) Convection

C) Radiation

D) Evaporation

20. Topic: Optics

Question 20: What does a convex lens do to parallel rays of light?

A) Disperses them

B) Focuses them at a point

C) Reflects them

D) Absorbs them

21. Topic: Electricity

Question 21: What is the unit of electrical resistance?

A) Volt

B) Ampere

C) Ohm

D) Watt

22. Topic: Magnetism

Question 22: Which of the following materials is not a good conductor of magnetic fields?

A) Iron

B) Copper

C) Nickel

D) Cobalt

Section 1: The Army Aviation Information Test

23. Topic: Aerodynamics

Question 23: What term describes the angle between the chord line and the oncoming air?

A) Angle of Attack

B) Angle of Incidence

C) Yaw Angle

D) Pitch Angle

24. Topic: Flight Controls

Question 24: What do flaps primarily assist with?

A) Rolling

B) Climbing

C) Landing

D) Banking

25. Topic: Weight and Balance

Question 25: What is the point called where all weight is balanced on an aircraft?

A) Datum

B) Center of Pressure

C) Center of Gravity

D) Aerodynamic Center

26. Topic: Basic Maneuvers

Question 26: What is a barrel roll a combination of?

A) Roll and Yaw

B) Roll and Pitch

C) Pitch and Yaw

D) Climb and Descent

Section 2: The Reading Comprehension Test

27. Topic: Strategies

Question 27: What should you do when encountering unfamiliar words in a passage?

A) Skip them

B) Guess their meaning

C) Use context clues

D) Look them up immediately

28. Topic: General Reading Comprehension Skills

Question 28: In a passage, where are supporting details most likely found?

A) Beginning

B) Middle

C) End

D) The details are scattered

Section 3: The Math Skills Test

29. Topic: Operations

Question 29: What is $3^2 - 4$?

A) 5

B) 9

C) -1

D) 7

30. Topic: Positive and Negative Numbers

Question 30: What is -3×-4?

A) 12

B) -12

C) -7

D) 7

31. Topic: Factors and Multiples

Question 31: What is the least common multiple of 3 and 4?

A) 6

B) 7

C) 12

D) 13

32. Topic: Systems of Equations

Question 32: If $2x+y=8$ and $x-y=2$, what is y?

A) 2

B) 3

C) 4

D) 5

33. Topic: Polynomial Algebra

Question 33: What is the simplified form of $(3x-2)^2$?

A) $9x^2-12x+4$

B) $9x^2-6x+4$

C) $6x^2-12x+4$

D) $9x^2+4$

34. Topic: Solving Quadratic Equations

Question 34: What is one root of $x^2+4x+4=0$?

A) -4

B) -2

C) 2

D) 4

35. Topic: Basic Geometry

Question 35: What is the perimeter of a square with a side length of 5 units?

A) 10

B) 15

C) 20

D) 25

Section 4: The Mechanical Comprehension Test

36. Topic: Kinetics

Question 36: What does Newton's Second Law of Motion describe?

A) Inertia

B) Acceleration

C) Momentum

D) Gravity

37. Topic: Work/Energy

Question 37: How is mechanical advantage calculated for an inclined plane?

A) Length/Height

B) Height/Length

C) Length x Height

D) Length - Height

38. Topic: Machines

Question 38: In a pulley system, what happens to the effort required as more pulleys are added?

A) Increases

B) Decreases

C) Stays the same

D) Becomes zero

39. Topic: Momentum/Impulse

Question 39: How is impulse related to change in momentum?

A) Impulse = Mass x Velocity

B) Impulse = Mass x Change in Velocity

C) Impulse = Force x Time

D) Impulse = Mass x Acceleration

40. Topic: Fluids

Question 40: What does the Pascal's law state about fluids?

A) Pressure increases with depth

B) Pressure is inversely proportional to area

C) Pressure applied at any point is transmitted undiminished in all directions

D) Pressure decreases with speed

41. Topic: Heat Transfer

Question 41: What is convection primarily involved in?

A) Solids

B) Liquids

C) Gases

D) Both Liquids and Gases

42. Topic: Optics

Question 42: What type of lens would you use to correct myopia?

A) Convex

B) Concave

C) Plano-Concave

D) Plano-Convex

43. Topic: Electricity

Question 43: What is the relationship between voltage (V), current (I), and resistance (R) described by Ohm's law?

A) $V=IR$

B) $V=I/R$

C) $I=VR$

D) $R=IV$

44. Topic: Magnetism

Question 44: What property allows a material to maintain its magnetic alignment even when the magnetizing field is removed?

A) Diamagnetism

B) Ferromagnetism

C) Paramagnetism

D) Antiferromagnetism

Section 1: The Army Aviation Information Test

45. Topic: Aerodynamics

Question 45: Which force opposes an aircraft's motion through the air?

A) Lift

B) Drag

C) Thrust

D) Gravity

46. Topic: Flight Controls

Question 46: What control surface is primarily responsible for pitch?

A) Ailerons

B) Elevators

C) Rudders

D) Flaps

47. Topic: Weight and Balance

Question 47: What term refers to the maximum weight an aircraft can safely carry?

A) Maximum Gross Weight

B) Maximum Cargo Weight

C) Center of Gravity

D) Dead Weight

48. Topic: Basic Maneuvers

Question 48: Which maneuver involves a steep climb followed by a loop?

A) Split-S

B) Immelmann

C) Cuban Eight

D) Chandelle

Section 2: The Reading Comprehension Test

49. Topic: Strategies

Question 49: What should you primarily look for when skimming a passage?

A) Details

B) Main Ideas

C) Supporting Ideas

D) Vocabulary

50. Topic: General Reading Comprehension Skills

Question 50: What does an author's tone refer to?

A) The pace of the story

B) The author's attitude toward the subject

C) The setting

D) The climax of the story

Section 3: The Math Skills Test

51. Topic: Operations

Question 51: What is 15×17?

A) 157

B) 235

C) 245

D) 255

52. Topic: Positive and Negative Numbers

Question 52: What is 4−7?

A) -3

B) 3

C) 11

D) -11

53. Topic: Factors and Multiples

Question 53: What is the greatest common factor of 16 and 24?

A) 4

B) 8

C) 2

D) 6

54. Topic: Systems of Equations Question 54: If $x+2y=10$ and $3x−y=4$, what is x?

A) 2

B) 3

C) 4

D) 5

55. Topic: Polynomial Algebra

Question 55: What is the simplified form of x^2-4?

A) x^2-4

B) $(x-2)(x+2)$

C) $(x-2)^2$

D) x^2+4

56. Topic: Solving Quadratic Equations

Question 56: What is a root of $x^2-x-6=0$?

A) -2

B) 2

C) 3

D) -3

57. Topic: Basic Geometry

Question 57: What is the area of a rectangle with a length of 4 units and a width of 3 units?

A) 12

B) 7

C) 14

D) 24

Section 4: The Mechanical Comprehension Test

58. Topic: Kinetics

Question 58: What term describes the change in position of an object with respect to time?

A) Acceleration

B) Displacement

C) Velocity

D) Momentum

59. Topic: Work/Energy

Question 59: What unit is used to measure work?

A) Joule

B) Newton

C) Watt

D) Ampere

60. Topic: Machines

Question 60: What machine consists of a wheel with a groove and a rope?

A) Lever

B) Pulley

C) Inclined Plane

D) Screw

61. Topic: Momentum/Impulse

Question 61: What is the momentum of an object with a mass of 3 kg moving at a speed of 4 m/s?

A) 7 kg.m/s

B) 12 kg.m/s

C) 1 kg.m/s

D) 24 kg.m/s

62. Topic: Fluids

Question 62: When a ship floats in water, which factor determines its buoyancy according to Archimedes' Principle?

A) Ship's weight

B) Ship's volume

C) Ship's density

D) Ship's velocity

63. Topic: Heat Transfer

Question 63: Which method of heat transfer does not require a medium?

A) Conduction

B) Convection

C) Radiation

D) Evaporation

64. Topic: Optics

Question 64: What type of mirror produces an upright, smaller image?

A) Convex

B) Concave

C) Plane

D) Parabolic

65. Topic: Electricity

Question 65: What does a capacitor store?

A) Current

B) Resistance

C) Voltage

D) Energy

66. Topic: Magnetism

Question 66: Which planet has the strongest magnetic field in our solar system?

A) Mars

B) Earth

C) Jupiter

D) Venus

Section 1: The Army Aviation Information Test

67. Topic: Aerodynamics

Question 67: What is ground effect in aviation?

A) A decrease in drag

B) An increase in lift

C) A decrease in lift

D) A decrease in thrust

68. Topic: Flight Controls

Question 68: Which instrument indicates an aircraft's altitude?

A) Airspeed Indicator

B) Altimeter

C) Gyroscope

D) VOR Indicator

69. Topic: Weight and Balance

Question 69: What is the point where all the weight is considered to be concentrated?

A) Balance Point

B) Center of Gravity

C) Datum Line

D) Longitudinal Axis

70. Topic: Basic Maneuvers

Question 70: Which of the following maneuvers involves reversing the direction of flight?

A) Barrel Roll

B) Loop

C) Chandelle

D) Hammerhead Turn

Section 2: The Reading Comprehension Test

71. Topic: Strategies

Question 71: What does it mean to infer something while reading?

A) To find the main idea

B) To draw a conclusion

C) To find details

D) To summarize the text

72. Topic: General Reading Comprehension Skills

Question 72: What is an antonym for "benevolent"?

A) Kind

B) Malevolent

C) Generous

D) Charitable

Section 3: The Math Skills Test

73. Topic: Operations

Question 73: What is 12^3?

A) 1548

B) 1678

C) 1728

D) 1758

74. Topic: Positive and Negative Numbers

Question 74: What is -2×-3?

A) -6

B) -1

C) 1

D) 6

75. Topic: Factors and Multiples

Question 75: What is the smallest multiple of 3 that is greater than 10?

A) 9

B) 12

C) 15

D) 18

76. Topic: Systems of Equations

Question 76: If $2x-y=4$ and $x+y=6$, what is y?

A) 1

B) 2

C) 3

D) 4

77. Topic: Polynomial Algebra

Question 77: What is the simplified form of $(x+2)^2$?

A) x^2+4

B) x^2+4x+4

C) x^2+2x+2

D) x^2+2x

78. Topic: Solving Quadratic Equations

Question 78: What is a root of $x^2+x-12=0$?

A) -4

B) 3

C) 4

D) -3

79. Topic: Basic Geometry

Question 79: What is the perimeter of a square with a side length of 4?

A) 12

B) 16

C) 8

D) 20

Section 4: The Mechanical Comprehension Test

80. Topic: Kinetics

Question 80: Which formula represents Newton's second law of motion, relating force, mass, and acceleration?

A) $F=ma$

B) $E=mc^2$

C) $P=mv$

D) $W=mg$

81. Topic: Work/Energy

Question 81: How much work is done when lifting a 2 kg weight to a height of 3 meters against gravity?

A) 2 J

B) 6 J

C) 12 J

D) 24 J

82. Topic: Machines

Question 82: What is the mechanical advantage of a lever with an effort arm of 4 meters and a resistance arm of 2 meters?

A) 0.5

B) 1

C) 2

D) 4

83. Topic: Momentum/Impulse

Question 83: What is the impulse delivered to a 5 kg object accelerating from 0 to 20 m/s?

A) 25 kg.m/s

B) 50 kg.m/s

C) 100 kg.m/s

D) 200 kg.m/s

84. Topic: Fluids

Question 84: What is the buoyancy force experienced by an object submerged in water with a volume of 2 m^3?

A) 2 N

B) 20 N

C) 19620 N

D) 39240 N

85. Topic: Heat Transfer

Question 85: In which state of matter is conduction least effective?

A) Solid

B) Liquid

C) Gas

D) Plasma

86. Topic: Optics

Question 86: What is the focal length of a convex lens with a power of 2 Diopters?

A) 0.5 m

B) 1 m

C) 2 m

D) 4 m

87. Topic: Electricity

Question 87: What is the resistance in a circuit with a voltage of 10V and a current of 2A?

A) 5 ohms

B) 20 ohms

C) 12 ohms

D) 8 ohms

88. Topic: Magnetism

Question 88: What is the unit of magnetic field strength?

A) Tesla

B) Gauss

C) Weber

D) Henry

Section 1: The Army Aviation Information Test

89. Topic: Aerodynamics

Question 89: What term refers to the angle between the chord line and the oncoming airflow?

A) Angle of Attack

B) Critical Angle

C) Angle of Incidence

D) Glide Slope

90. Topic: Flight Controls

Question 90: What control surface adjusts an aircraft's roll?

A) Rudder

B) Elevator

C) Ailerons

D) Flaps

91. Topic: Weight and Balance

Question 91: What is the purpose of ballast in an aircraft?

A) Increase Lift

B) Improve Balance

C) Increase Speed

D) Improve Fuel Efficiency

92. Topic: Basic Maneuvers

Question 92: What maneuver allows the pilot to lose altitude quickly without gaining airspeed?

A) Slip

B) Stall

C) Dive

D) Spin

Section 2: The Reading Comprehension Test

93. Topic: Strategies

Question 93: What is the term for a question that asks you to identify the author's opinion?

A) Inferential question

B) Literal question

C) Evaluative question

D) Analytical question

94. Topic: General Reading Comprehension Skills

Question 94: What does the term "context clues" refer to?

A) Background information

B) Words surrounding a difficult word

C) Textual themes

D) Author's biography

Section 3: The Math Skills Test

95. Topic: Operations

Question 95: What is $9-2\times3+5$?

A) 10

B) 4

C) 8

D) 20

96. Topic: Positive and Negative Numbers

Question 96: What is $-4-(-6)$?

A) -10

B) -2

C) 2

D) 10

97. Topic: Factors and Multiples

Question 97: Which of the following is a factor of 24?

A) 5

B) 7

C) 8

D) 11

98. Topic: Systems of Equations

Question 98: If $3x+4y=12$ and $x-y=2$, what is x?

A) 3

B) 4

C) 2

D) 5

99. Topic: Polynomial Algebra

Question 99: What is the simplified form of $2x(x-5)+3$?

A) $2x^2-10x+3$

B) $2x^2-15$

C) $2x^2+3x-15$

D) x^2-5x+6

100. Topic: Solving Quadratic Equations

Question 100: What is one root of $x^2-4=0$?

A) -2

B) 0

C) 1

D) 2

5.2 ANSWER SHEET – PRACTICE TEST 1

1. Answer: C)

Explanation: Lift is affected by factors like airspeed, altitude, and air density, but the color of the aircraft is irrelevant to aerodynamics.

2. Answer: A)

Explanation: Ailerons are primarily used to control the roll of an aircraft.

3. Answer: C)

Explanation: An aircraft that is tail-heavy is generally unstable and hard to control.

4. Answer: B)

Explanation: Generally, airspeed decreases during a climb due to increased angle of attack and drag.

5. Answer: D)

Explanation: Close reading of the passage is the most effective strategy for tackling inference-based questions.

6. Answer: A)

Explanation: The main idea is generally found at the beginning of a passage.

7. Answer: A)

Explanation: According to the order of operations, you first multiply 3 by 2, which is 6. Then, add 5 to get 11.

8. Answer: B)

Explanation: In the realm of negative numbers, -3 is smaller than -2.

9. Answer: D)

Explanation: A factor divides the given number without a remainder. 36 divided by 12 gives a whole number.

10. Answer: B)

Explanation: Adding the two equations eliminates y, giving $2x=6$, which means $x=3$. Substituting this into one of the equations gives $y=2$.

11. Answer: A)

Explanation: Expanding $(x+2)(x+2)$ gives x^2+4x+4.

12. Answer: A)

Explanation: Factoring the equation x^2-3x+2 gives $(x-1)(x-2)=0$. Therefore, the roots are 1,2.

13. Answer: B)

Explanation: The sum of interior angles in a triangle is always 180 degrees.

14. Answer: A)

Explanation: The formula for kinetic energy is $KE=1/2\ mv^2$.

15. Answer: B)

Explanation: The unit of work is the Joule (J), which is equivalent to a Newton-meter (Nm).

16. Answer: C)

Explanation: Mechanical Advantage = Effort Arm / Load Arm = 4m / 2m = 2.

17. Answer: C)

Explanation: Momentum = mass x velocity = 5 kg x 3 m/s = 15 Ns.

18. Answer: B)

Explanation: Archimedes' Principle explains that an object submerged in a fluid experiences an upward force equal to the weight of the fluid displaced.

19. Answer: C)

Explanation: Radiation from the Sun is the primary method of heat transfer responsible for heating the Earth's surface.

20. Answer: B)

Explanation: A convex lens focuses parallel rays of light at a single point.

21. Answer: C)

Explanation: The unit of electrical resistance is the Ohm.

22. Answer: B)

Explanation: Copper is not a good conductor of magnetic fields; it is primarily used as an electrical conductor.

23. Answer: A)

Explanation: The angle of attack is the angle between the chord line of the airfoil and the oncoming air.

24. Answer: C)

Explanation: Flaps are primarily used to increase lift during landing, allowing for a slower approach speed.

25. Answer: C)

Explanation: The center of gravity is the point where the weight of an aircraft is balanced.

26. Answer: B)

Explanation: A barrel roll is a combination of roll and pitch.

27. Answer: C)

Explanation: Using context clues can help you infer the meaning of unfamiliar words, which is more time-efficient during a test.

28. Answer: B)

Explanation: Supporting details are most often found in the middle of a passage.

29. Answer: A)

Explanation: $3^2=9$, and $9-4=5$.

30. Answer: A)

Explanation: Negative multiplied by negative gives a positive result. $-3\times-4=12$.

31. Answer: C)

Explanation: The least common multiple of 3 and 4 is 12.

32. Answer: B)

Explanation: Solving the system of equations, you get $y=3$.

33. Answer: A)

Explanation: Expanding $(3x-2)(3x-2)$ gives $9x^2-12x+4$.

34. Answer: B)

Explanation: Factoring gives $(x+2)^2=0$, so one root is $x=-2$.

35. Answer: C)

Explanation: Perimeter of a square is 4×side length, which is 4×5=20 units.

36. Answer: B)

Explanation: Newton's Second Law describes how the velocity of an object changes when subjected to an external force, essentially describing acceleration.

37. Answer: A)

Explanation: Mechanical advantage for an inclined plane is calculated by Length/Height.

38. Answer: B)

Explanation: As more pulleys are added to the system, the effort required to lift a weight decreases.

39. Answer: C)

Explanation: Impulse is equal to the change in momentum and is calculated as Impulse=Force×Time.

40. Answer: C)

Explanation: Pascal's law states that pressure applied at any point in an incompressible fluid is transmitted undiminished in all directions.

41. Answer: D)

Explanation: Convection is primarily involved in heat transfer through fluids, which include both liquids and gases.

42. Answer: B)

Explanation: A concave lens is used to correct myopia or nearsightedness.

43. Answer: A)

Explanation: Ohm's law describes the relationship as $V=IR$.

44. Answer: B)

Explanation: Ferromagnetism is the property that allows a material to maintain its magnetic alignment even when the magnetizing field is removed.

45. Answer: B)

Explanation: Drag opposes an aircraft's motion through the air.

46. Answer: B)

Explanation: Elevators are primarily responsible for controlling pitch.

47. Answer: A)

Explanation: The maximum weight an aircraft can safely carry is referred to as its Maximum Gross Weight.

48. Answer: B)

Explanation: An Immelmann involves a steep climb followed by a loop.

49. Answer: B)

Explanation: When skimming a passage, you should primarily look for the main ideas.

50. Answer: B)

Explanation: The author's tone refers to their attitude toward the subject.

51. Answer: D)

Explanation: 15×17=255.

52. Answer: A)

Explanation: 4−7=−3.

53. Answer: B)

Explanation: The greatest common factor of 16 and 24 is 8.

54. Answer: B)

Explanation: Solving the system of equations gives $x=3$.

55. Answer: B)

Explanation: x^2-4 can be factored into $(x-2)(x+2)$.

56. Answer: C)

Explanation: Factoring gives $(x-3)(x+2)=0$, so one root is $x=3$.

57. Answer: A)

Explanation: The area of a rectangle is Length×Width=4×3=12.

58. Answer: C)

Explanation: Velocity describes the change in position of an object with respect to time.

59. Answer: A)

Explanation: Work is measured in Joules.

60. Answer: B)

Explanation: A pulley consists of a wheel with a groove and a rope.

61. Answer: B)

Explanation: Momentum is calculated as Mass×Velocity=3 kg×4 m/s=12 kg. m/s.

62. Answer: B)

Explanation: According to Archimedes' Principle, the buoyant force acting on a ship is determined by the volume of water displaced by the submerged part of the ship.

63. Answer: C)

Explanation: Radiation is the method of heat transfer that does not require a medium.

64. Answer: A)

Explanation: A convex mirror produces an upright, smaller image.

65. Answer: D)

Explanation: A capacitor stores energy in an electric field.

66. Answer: C)

Explanation: Jupiter has the strongest magnetic field in our solar system.

67. Answer: B)

Explanation: Ground effect in aviation refers to an increase in lift close to the ground.

68. Answer: B)

Explanation: An altimeter indicates an aircraft's altitude.

69. Answer: B)

Explanation: The point where all the weight is considered to be concentrated is known as the Center of Gravity.

70. Answer: D)

Explanation: A Hammerhead Turn involves reversing the direction of flight.

71. Answer: B)

Explanation: Inferring means drawing a conclusion based on information given.

72. Answer: B)

Explanation: An antonym for "benevolent" is "malevolent."

73. Answer: C)

Explanation: $12^3 = 1728$.

74. Answer: D)

Explanation: $-2 \times -3 = 6$.

75. Answer: B)

Explanation: The smallest multiple of 3 greater than 10 is 12.

76. Answer: A)

Explanation: Solving the system of equations gives $y=1$.

77. Answer: B)

Explanation: The simplified form of $(x+2)^2$ is x^2+4x+4.

78. Answer: D)

Explanation: Factoring gives $(x-3)(x+4)=0$, so one root is $x=-4$.

79. Answer: B)

Explanation: The perimeter of a square is $4 \times$ Side length$=4 \times 4=16$.

80. Answer: A)

Explanation: Newton's second law states that the force (F) acting on an object is equal to the mass (m) of the object multiplied by its acceleration (a).

81. Answer: D)

Explanation: Work is calculated as $Work=mgh=2 \times 9.81 \times 3=58.86 \approx 59J$.

82. Answer: C)

Explanation: The mechanical advantage is $Effort\ Arm\ /\ Resistance\ Arm=4/2=2$.

83. Answer: C)

Explanation: Impulse is calculated as $Impulse=\Delta p=m \Delta v=5 \times 20=100 kg.m/s$.

84. Answer: D)

Explanation: Buoyancy force is calculated as $FB = \rho \times g \times V = 1000 \times 9.81 \times 2 = 19620 \times 2 = 39240N$.

85. Answer: C)

Explanation: Conduction is least effective in gases due to the large spacing between particles.

86. Answer: A)

Explanation: Focal length $f = 1/Power = 1/2 = 0.5m$.

87. Answer: A)

Explanation: Resistance $R = V/I = 10/2 = 5$ ohms.

88. Answer: A)

Explanation: The unit of magnetic field strength is Tesla.

89. Answer: A)

Explanation: The angle between the chord line and the oncoming airflow is called the Angle of Attack.

90. Answer: C)

Explanation: Ailerons are used to control the roll of an aircraft.

91. Answer: B)

Explanation: The purpose of ballast in an aircraft is to improve balance.

92. Answer: A)

Explanation: A slip allows the pilot to lose altitude quickly without gaining airspeed.

93. Answer: C)

Explanation: An Evaluative question asks you to identify the author's opinion.

94. Answer: B)

Explanation: Context clues refer to words surrounding a difficult word that can help you understand its meaning.

95. Answer: C)

Explanation: $9-2\times3+5=9-6+5=3+5=8$.

96. Answer: C)

Explanation: $-4-(-6)=-4+6=2$.

97. Answer: C)

Explanation: 8 is a factor of 24 because 24 can be evenly divided by 8.

98. Answer: A)

Explanation: Solving the system of equations gives $x=3$.

99. Answer: A)

Explanation: The simplified form is $2x^2-10x+3$.

100. Answer: D)

Explanation: Factoring gives $(x-2)(x+2)=0$, so one root is $x=2$.

6.1 FULL-LENGTH PRACTICE TEST 2

Section 1: The Army Aviation Information Test

101. Topic: Aerodynamics

Question 101: What does the term "stall speed" refer to?

A) Maximum speed

B) Minimum lift speed

C) Minimum speed before stall occurs

D) Speed during landing

102. Topic: Flight Controls Question

102: What is the function of the yaw axis?

A) Pitch

B) Roll

C) Yaw

D) Altitude

103. Topic: Weight and Balance

Question 103: What term describes the point where all weight is balanced?

A) Aerodynamic Center

B) Center of Gravity

C) Fulcrum Point

D) Balance Beam

104. Topic: Basic Maneuvers

Question 104: What maneuver involves both a roll and a pitch?

A) Loop

B) Barrel Roll

C) Split S

D) Immelmann Turn

Section 2: The Reading Comprehension Test

105. Topic: Strategies

Question 105: Which technique involves reading the first and last sentences of a paragraph to grasp the main idea?

A) Skimming

B) Scanning

C) Meta-cognition

D) Annotating

106. Topic: General Reading Comprehension Skills

Question 106: What term refers to the main idea or message in a text?

A) Theme

B) Summary

C) Argument

D) Opinion

Section 3: The Math Skills Test

107. Topic: Operations

Question 107: What is 5^3?

A) 125

B) 15

C) 60

D) 25

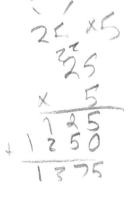

108. Topic: Positive and Negative Numbers

Question 108: What is $-3+8$?

A) -5

B) -11

C) 5

D) 11

109. Topic: Factors and Multiples

Question 109: What is the smallest multiple of 7 greater than 50?

A) 51

B) 56

C) 49

D) 57

110. Topic: Systems of Equations

Question 110: If $x+y=10$ and $2x-y=4$, what is y?

A) 2

B) 3

133

C) 4

D) 6

111. Topic: Polynomial Algebra

Question 111: What is the simplified form of $x(x+4)-2$?

$x^2 + 4x - 2$

A) x^2+4x-2

B) x^2-2x+8

C) x^2-2x+2

D) x^2+2x-8

112. Topic: Solving Quadratic Equations

Question 112: What is one root of $x^2+4x+4=0$?

A) -2

B) 0

C) 2

D) 4

113. Topic: Basic Geometry

Question 113: What is the sum of the angles in a quadrilateral?

A) 90 degrees

B) 180 degrees

C) 270 degrees

D) 360 degrees

Section 4: The Mechanical Comprehension Test

114. Topic: Kinetics

Question 114: What is Newton's first law of motion also known as?

A) Law of Inertia

B) Law of Acceleration

C) Law of Action-Reaction

D) Law of Gravitation

115. Topic: Work/Energy

Question 115: What is the unit of work in the SI system?

A) Joule

B) Watt

C) Newton

D) Ampere

116. Topic: Machines

Question 116: What is the mechanical advantage of a lever with an effort arm of 6m and a load arm of 2m?

A) 3

B) 4

C) 1

D) 2

117. Topic: Momentum/Impulse

Question 117: What is the impulse given to an object if the force acting on it is 5 N for 3 seconds?

A) 2 Ns

B) 8 Ns

C) 15 Ns

D) 16 Ns

118. Topic: Fluids

Question 118: If an object is fully submerged in a fluid and experiences a buoyant force greater than its weight, what will happen to the object?

A) Sink

B) Float

C) Remain stationary

D) Disintegrate

119. Topic: Heat Transfer

Question 119: Which mode of heat transfer involves the movement of fluids?

A) Conduction

B) Convection

C) Radiation

D) Reflection

120. Topic: Optics

Question 120: What type of lens makes objects appear smaller?

A) Convex

B) Concave

C) Plano-convex

D) Plano-concave

121. Topic: Electricity

Question 121: What is the unit of electrical resistance?

A) Ohm

B) Ampere

C) Volt

D) Watt

122. Topic: Magnetism

Question 122: What type of material is not attracted to a magnet?

A) Ferromagnetic

B) Paramagnetic

C) Diamagnetic

D) Non-magnetic

Section 1: The Army Aviation Information Test

123. Topic: Aerodynamics

Question 123: What is the effect of increasing altitude on air density?

A) Increases

B) Decreases

C) Remains the same

D) Varies unpredictably

124. Topic: Flight Controls

Question 124: What is the primary function of flaps on an airplane?

A) Increase speed

B) Decrease speed

C) Increase lift

D) Decrease lift

125. Topic: Weight and Balance

Question 125: How is payload different from the gross weight of an aircraft?

A) Includes fuel

B) Excludes fuel

C) Includes passengers

D) Excludes passengers

126. Topic: Basic Maneuvers

Question 126: What is the aerobatic maneuver that involves an airplane making a 360-degree roll?

A) Aileron roll

B) Loop

C) Cuban Eight

D) Snap roll

Section 2: The Reading Comprehension Test

127. Topic: Strategies

Question 127: What is the purpose of using context clues in reading?

A) To predict the ending

B) To understand unfamiliar words

C) To identify the main characters

D) To critique the author's style

128. Topic: General Reading Comprehension Skills

Question 128: What is an inference?

A) A stated fact

B) An educated guess

C) An irrelevant detail

D) A dialogue tag

Section 3: The Math Skills Test

129. Topic: Operations

Question 129: What is 17×18?

A) 286

B) 296

Ⓒ 306

D) 316

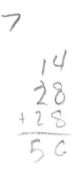

130. Topic: Positive and Negative Numbers

Question 130: What is the value of -5×-5?

A) -25

B) 0

Ⓒ 25

D) -10

131. Topic: Factors and Multiples

Question 131: Which of the following numbers is not a multiple of 4?

A) 12

B) 16

C) 20

D) 22

132. Topic: Systems of Equations

Question 132: If $2x+y=10$ and $x-2y=4$, what is x?

A) 2

B) 4

C) 6

D) 8

133. Topic: Polynomial Algebra

Question 133: What is the simplified form of $2x(x-5)+3$?

A) $2x^2-10x+3$

B) $2x^2+3x-15$

C) x^2-5x+6

D) $2x^2+10x+3$

134. Topic: Solving Quadratic Equations

Question 134: What are the roots of $x^2 - 4x + 4 = 0$?

A) -2 and -2

B) 0 and 4

C) 2 and 2

D) 0 and 0

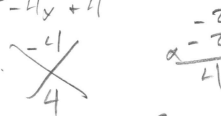

135. Topic: Basic Geometry

Question 135: What is the area of a rectangle with a length of 4 and a width of 6?

A) 20

B) 24

C) 28

D) 40

Section 4: The Mechanical Comprehension Test

136. Topic: Kinetics

Question 136: What term describes the force exerted by a moving object?

A) Inertia

B) Momentum

C) Friction

D) Acceleration

137. Topic: Work/Energy

Question 137: What form of energy is stored in a compressed spring?

A) Thermal

B) Kinetic

C) Potential

D) Chemical

138. Topic: Machines

Question 138: What do you call a simple machine consisting of a wheel with a groove in it for a rope?

A) Lever

B) Pulley

C) Screw

D) Wedge

139. Topic: Momentum/Impulse

Question 139: What is the momentum of a 2 kg object moving at 3 m/s?

A) 5 kgm/s

B) 6 kgm/s

C) 8 kgm/s

D) 10 kgm/s

140. Topic: Fluids

Question 140: What principle states that the pressure in a fluid decreases as the fluid's velocity increases?

A) Pascal's Principle

B) Archimedes' Principle

C) Bernoulli's Principle

D) Newton's Third Law

141. Topic: Heat Transfer

Question 141: What is the transfer of heat through electromagnetic waves?

A) Conduction

B) Convection

C) Radiation

D) Reflection

142. Topic: Optics

Question 142: What does a red filter do to white light?

A) Absorbs all colors except red

B) Reflects all colors except red

C) Absorbs red and allows other colors to pass

D) Reflects red and absorbs other colors

143. Topic: Electricity

Question 143: Which of the following is a good insulator?

A) Copper

B) Aluminum

C) Rubber

D) Iron

144. Topic: Magnetism

Question 144: What type of magnetism is exhibited by materials that are weakly attracted to magnets?

A) Ferromagnetic

B) Paramagnetic

C) Diamagnetic

D) Non-magnetic

Section 1: The Army Aviation Information Test

145. Topic: Aerodynamics

Question 145: What effect does an increase in wing area have on lift?

A) Increases

B) Decreases

C) Remains the same

D) Varies unpredictably

146. Topic: Flight Controls

Question 146: What is the function of the rudder in flight?

A) Roll control

B) Pitch control

C) Yaw control

D) Altitude control

147. Topic: Weight and Balance

Question 147: Which of the following increases stability in an aircraft?

A) Lower center of gravity

B) Higher center of gravity

C) Increased speed

D) Reduced speed

148. Topic: Basic Maneuvers

Question 148: Which maneuver involves flying the airplane in a U-shape pattern?

A) Chandelle

B) Split-S

C) Immelmann

D) Lazy Eight

Section 2: The Reading Comprehension Test

149. Topic: Strategies

Question 149: Which of the following is a pre-reading strategy?

A) Summarizing

B) Skimming

C) Inferring

D) Visualizing

150. Topic: General Reading Comprehension Skills

Question 150: Which of the following details is often the least important in a narrative?

A) Setting

B) Main idea

C) Minor characters

D) Conflict

Section 3: The Math Skills Test

151. Topic: Operations

Question 151: What is 2492/14?

A) 158

149

B) 168

C) 178

D) 188

152. Topic: Positive and Negative Numbers

Question 152: What is the sum of +3 and −7?

A) −4   −4

B) +4

C) −10

D) +10

153. Topic: Factors and Multiples

Question 153: What is the smallest positive multiple of 3 that is greater than 14?

A) 9   3

B) 12   6

C) 15   9

D) 18   12

154. Topic: Systems of Equations

Question 154: If $x+y=10$ and $x-y=2$, what is y?

A) 3

B) 4

C) 5

D) 6

$$(x + y = 10)^-$$
$$x - y = 2$$

$$-x - y = -10$$
$$x - y = 2$$

$$-2y = -8$$
$$y = 4$$

155. Topic: Polynomial Algebra

Question 155: What is the simplified form of $3x(x+4)-2$?

A) $3x^2+12x-2$

B) $3x^2-12x+2$

C) x^2+4x-6

D) $3x^2+12x+2$

156. Topic: Solving Quadratic Equations

Question 156: What are the roots of $x^2+4x+4=0$?

A) $-4,-4$

B) $-2,-2$

C) $2,2$

D) $0,0$

151

157. Topic: Basic Geometry

Question 157: What is the perimeter of a square with a side length of 6?

A) 10

B) 20

C) 24

D) 15

Section 4: The Mechanical Comprehension Test

158. Topic: Kinetics Question

158: What is the unit of force in the International System of Units?

A) Joule

B) Newton

C) Watt

D) Pascal

159. Topic: Work/Energy

Question 159: What is the term for energy in motion?

A) Potential energy

B) Kinetic energy

C) Thermal energy

D) Chemical energy

160. Topic: Machines

Question 160: What is the mechanical advantage of a lever with an effort arm of 4 meters and a resistance arm of 2 meters?

A) 0.5

B) 1

C) 2

D) 4

161. Topic: Momentum/Impulse

Question 161: What is the impulse experienced by an object if a force of 5 N acts on it for 2 seconds?

A) 2.5 Ns

B) 5 Ns

C) 7.5 Ns

D) 10 Ns

162. Topic: Fluids

Question 162: What is the primary cause of buoyancy?

A) Heat

B) Gravity

C) Air pressure

D) Pressure difference in fluids

163. Topic: Heat Transfer

Question 163: Which method of heat transfer is responsible for the warmth you feel from the sun or a heated object without direct contact?

A) Conduction

B) Convection

C) Radiation

D) Insulation

164. Topic: Optics

Question 164: What is the focal length of a convex lens?

A) Positive

B) Negative

C) Zero

D) Undefined

165. Topic: Electricity

Question 165: What does Ohm's Law describe?

A) Resistance

B) Current

C) Voltage

D) Relationship between Voltage, Current, and Resistance

166. Topic: Magnetism

Question 166: What happens to a ferromagnetic material when it is magnetized?

A) It loses its magnetism

B) Its domains align

C) It becomes an insulator

D) Its electrical conductivity increases

Section 1: The Army Aviation Information Test

167. Topic: Aerodynamics

Question 167: What is the term for the angle between the wing and the airflow?

A) Angle of attack

B) Aspect ratio

C) Camber

D) Washout

168. Topic: Flight Controls

Question 168: Which of these controls the pitch of an aircraft?

A) Ailerons

B) Elevators

C) Rudder

D) Flaps

169. Topic: Weight and Balance

Question 169: What does exceeding the gross weight limit affect?

A) Lift only

B) Drag only

C) Both lift and drag

D) Neither lift nor drag

170. Topic: Basic Maneuvers

Question 170: What is a "stall" in aviation?

A) Rapid descent

B) Loss of lift

C) Sudden acceleration

D) Sudden stop

Section 2: The Reading Comprehension Test

171. Topic: Strategies

Question 171: Which strategy involves making educated guesses about a text's content?

A) Previewing

B) Skimming

C) Scanning

D) Predicting

172. Topic: General Reading Comprehension Skills

Question 172: What does an author's tone refer to?

A) Structure

B) Perspective

C) Mood

D) Attitude

Section 3: The Math Skills Test

173. Topic: Operations

Question 173: What is 15^3?

A) 3155

B) 3285

C) 3375

D) 3395

174. Topic: Positive and Negative Numbers

Question 174: What is the sum of $+7$ and -10?

A) -3

B) $+3$

C) -17

D) +17

175. Topic: Factors and Multiples

Question 175: What are the factors of 12?

A) 1, 2, 3, 4

B) 1, 2, 4, 6, 12

C) 1, 2, 3, 6, 12

D) 1, 3, 6, 12

176. Topic: Systems of Equations

Question 176: If $2x+y=11$ and $x-y=3$, what is x?

A) 4

B) 5

C) 6

D) 7

177. Topic: Polynomial Algebra

Question 177: What is the simplified form of $5x(x-2)+3$?

A) $5x^2-10x+3$

B) $5x^2+10x-3$

C) $5x^2-10x-3$

D) $5x^2+10x+3$

178. Topic: Solving Quadratic Equations

Question 178: What are the roots of $x^2-5x+6=0$?

A) 2 and 3

B) -2 *and* -3

C) 2 and -3

D) -2 *and* 3

179. Topic: Basic Geometry

Question 179: What is the area of a triangle with a base of 5 and a height of 10?

A) 25

B) 50

C) 100

D) 200

Section 4: The Mechanical Comprehension Test

180. Topic: Kinetics

Question 180: What is the formula for calculating the potential energy (U) of an object in a gravitational field, considering mass (m) and height (h)?

A) $U=mgh$

B) $U=1/2mv^2$

C) $U=k*q_1q_2/r$

D) $U=-GM\,m/r$

181. Topic: Work/Energy

Question 181: What is the unit of work?

A) Watt

B) Newton

C) Joule

D) Ampere

182. Topic: Machines

Question 182: What is the ideal mechanical advantage of a ramp that is 10 meters long and 2 meters high?

A) 5

B) 10

C) 20

D) 50

183. Topic: Momentum/Impulse

Question 183: If an object at rest gains an impulse of 10 Ns, what will be its momentum?

A) 0 Ns

B) 5 Ns

C) 10 Ns

D) 20 Ns

184. Topic: Fluids

Question 184: What does Bernoulli's principle describe?

A) Heat transfer in fluids

B) Viscosity of fluids

C) Relationship between fluid speed and pressure

D) Buoyancy in fluids

185. Topic: Heat Transfer

Question 185: What is conduction?

A) Transfer of heat by electromagnetic waves

B) Transfer of heat by movement of particles

C) Transfer of heat through direct contact

D) Transfer of heat through radiation

186. Topic: Optics

Question 186: What does a concave lens do?

A) Converges light

B) Diverges light

C) Neither converges nor diverges light

D) Amplifies light

187. Topic: Electricity

Question 187: What is the unit of electrical charge?

A) Coulomb

B) Volt

C) Ampere

D) Ohm

188. Topic: Magnetism

Question 188: What is the magnetic field inside a solenoid described by?

A) Strength and direction

B) Strength and polarity

C) Polarity and direction

D) Strength, polarity, and direction

Section 1: The Army Aviation Information Test

189. Topic: Aerodynamics

Question 189: What is ground effect in aviation?

A) Reduced lift near the ground

B) Increased drag near the ground

C) Reduced drag near the ground

D) Increased lift near the ground

190. Topic: Flight Controls

Question 190: What are flaperons used for?

A) Increasing drag only

B) Increasing lift only

C) Both increasing lift and increasing drag

D) Neither increasing lift nor increasing drag

191. Topic: Weight and Balance

Question 191: What is ballast in aviation?

A) Extra fuel

B) Weight added for balance

C) Navigation equipment

D) Communications system

192. Topic: Basic Maneuvers

Question 192: What is a "barrel roll"?

A) A vertical loop

B) A 360-degree roll

C) A roll around a horizontal axis

D) A roll and climb combined

Section 2: The Reading Comprehension Test

193. Topic: Strategies

Question 193: What does inferencing involve?

A) Predicting the future

B) Making conclusions based on evidence

C) Speed reading

D) Identifying the main idea

194. Topic: General Reading Comprehension Skills

Question 194: What is a synonym?

A) A word with the opposite meaning

B) A word with the same meaning

C) A word with a similar sound

D) A word with the same spelling

Section 3: The Math Skills Test

195. Topic: Operations

Question 195: What is 7×9?

A) 56

B) 63

C) 66

D) 72

196. Topic: Positive and Negative Numbers

Question 196: What is $-5+9$?

A) 4

B) -4

C) 14

D) -14

197. Topic: Factors and Multiples

Question 197: What is the least common multiple (LCM) of 3 and 5?

A) 5

B) 8

C) 12

D) 15

198. Topic: Systems of Equations

Question 198: If $3x-2y=6$ and $x+y=5$, what is y?

A) 1

B) 2

C) 3

D) 4

199. Topic: Polynomial Algebra

Question 199: What is the simplified form of $2x(x+3)+5$?

A) $2x^2+6x+5$

B) $2x^2-6x+5$

C) $2x^2+6x-5$

D) $2x^2-6x-5$

200. Topic: Solving Quadratic Equations

Question 200: What is the discriminant of $x^2-3x+1=0$?

A) 1

B) 5

C) 9

D) 13

6.2 ANSWER SHEET – PRACTICE TEST 2

101. Answer: C)

Explanation: Stall speed is the minimum airspeed at which an aircraft can maintain controlled flight without stalling.

102. Answer: C)

Explanation: The yaw axis is responsible for the yaw motion of the aircraft, which is essentially the side-to-side movement around the vertical axis.

103. Answer: B)

Explanation: The point where all weight is balanced is known as the Center of Gravity.

104. Answer: B)

Explanation: A Barrel Roll involves both a roll and a pitch movement.

105. Answer: A)

Explanation: Skimming involves reading the first and last sentences of a paragraph to get the main idea.

106. Answer: A)

Explanation: The term "Theme" refers to the main idea or underlying message in a text.

107. Answer: A)

Explanation: $5^3=5\times5\times5=125$.

108. Answer: C)

Explanation: $-3+8=5$.

109. Answer: B)

Explanation: The smallest multiple of 7 greater than 50 is 56.

110. Answer: D)

Explanation: Solving the system of equations gives $y=6$.

111. Answer: A)

Explanation: The simplified form is x^2+4x-2.

112. Answer: A)

Explanation: Factoring gives $(x+2)^2=0$, so one root is $x=-2$.

113. Answer: D)

Explanation: The sum of the interior angles of a quadrilateral is always 360 degrees.

114. Answer: A)

Explanation: Newton's first law of motion is also known as the Law of Inertia.

115. Answer: A)

Explanation: The unit of work in the SI system is the Joule.

116. Answer: A)

Explanation: Mechanical Advantage = Effort arm / Load arm = 6m / 2m = 3.

117. Answer: C)

Explanation: Impulse = Force x Time = 5 N x 3 s = 15 Ns.

118. Answer: B)

- **Explanation**: If the buoyant force is greater than the weight of the object, the object will float.

119. Answer: B)

Explanation: Convection involves the movement of fluids for heat transfer.

120. Answer: B)

Explanation: A concave lens makes objects appear smaller.

121. Answer: A)

Explanation: The unit of electrical resistance is the Ohm.

122. Answer: D)

Explanation: Non-magnetic materials are not attracted to a magnet.

123. Answer: B)

Explanation: As altitude increases, air density decreases.

124. Answer: C)

Explanation: Flaps are primarily used to increase lift during takeoff and landing.

125. Answer: B)

Explanation: Payload excludes the weight of the fuel.

126. Answer: A)

Explanation: An aileron roll involves a 360-degree roll around the aircraft's longitudinal axis.

127. Answer: B)

Explanation: Context clues are used to understand unfamiliar words in a text.

128. Answer: B)

Explanation: An inference is an educated guess based on evidence in the text.

129. Answer: C)

Explanation: $17 \times 18 = 306$.

130. Answer: C)

Explanation: $-5 \times -5 = 25$.

131. Answer: D)

Explanation: 22 is not a multiple of 4.

132. Answer: C)

Explanation: Solving the system of equations gives $x=6$.

133. Answer: A)

Explanation: The simplified form is $2x^2-10x+3$.

134. Answer: C)

Explanation: Factoring gives $(x-2)^2=0$, so the roots are $x=2$ and $x=2$.

135. Answer: B)

Explanation: The area of the rectangle is $4\times6=24$.

136. Answer: B)

Explanation: Momentum describes the force exerted by a moving object.

137. Answer: C)

Explanation: The energy stored in a compressed spring is potential energy.

138. Answer: B)

Explanation: A wheel with a groove in it for a rope is a pulley.

139. Answer: B)

Explanation: Momentum = mass x velocity = $2kg\times3m/s=6kg\square m/s$.

140. Answer: C)

Explanation: Bernoulli's Principle states that the pressure in a fluid decreases as the fluid's velocity increases.

141. Answer: C)

Explanation: The transfer of heat through electromagnetic waves is called radiation.

142. Answer: A)

Explanation: A red filter absorbs all colors except red, which it allows to pass through.

143. Answer: C)

Explanation: Rubber is a good insulator of electricity.

144. Answer: B)

Explanation: Paramagnetic materials are weakly attracted to magnets.

145. Answer: A)

Explanation: Increasing wing area generally increases lift.

146. Answer: C)

Explanation: The rudder controls yaw.

147. Answer: A)

Explanation: A lower center of gravity increases stability.

148. Answer: D)

Explanation: A Lazy Eight involves flying the airplane in a U-shape pattern.

149. Answer: B)

Explanation: Skimming is often used as a pre-reading strategy to get an overview of the text.

150. Answer: C)

Explanation: Minor characters are often the least important in a narrative.

151. Answer: C)

Explanation: 2492/14=178.

152. Answer: A)

Explanation: +3+(−7)=−4.

153. Answer: C)

Explanation: 15 is the smallest positive multiple of 3 that is greater than 14.

154. Answer: B)

Explanation: Solving the system of equations gives $y=4$.

155. Answer: A)

Explanation: The simplified form is $3x^2+12x−2$.

156. Answer: B)

Explanation: Factoring gives $(x+2)^2=0$, so the roots are $x=−2$ and $x=−2$.

157. Answer: C)

Explanation: The perimeter of the square is 4×6=24.

158. Answer: B)

Explanation: The unit of force in the International System of Units is the Newton.

159. Answer: B)

Explanation: Energy in motion is referred to as kinetic energy.

160. Answer: C)

Explanation: Mechanical advantage = effort arm / resistance arm = 4m / 2m = 2.

161. Answer: D)

Explanation: Impulse = force x time = $5N \times 2s = 10Ns$.

162. Answer: D)

Explanation: The primary cause of buoyancy is the pressure difference in fluids.

163. Answer: C)

Explanation: Radiation is responsible for the transfer of heat without the need for direct contact, such as feeling the warmth from the sun.

164. Answer: A)

Explanation: The focal length of a convex lens is positive.

165. Answer: D)

Explanation: Ohm's Law describes the relationship between voltage, current, and resistance.

166. Answer: B)

Explanation: When a ferromagnetic material is magnetized, its domains align.

167. Answer: A)

Explanation: The angle between the wing and the airflow is known as the angle of attack.

168. Answer: B)

Explanation: The elevators control the pitch of an aircraft.

169. Answer: C)

Explanation: Exceeding the gross weight limit affects both lift and drag.

170. Answer: B)

Explanation: A stall in aviation refers to a loss of lift.

171. Answer: D)

Explanation: Predicting involves making educated guesses about a text's content.

172. Answer: D)

Explanation: An author's tone refers to their attitude toward the subject.

173. Answer: C)

Explanation: $15^3 = 3375$.

174. Answer: A)

Explanation: $+7+(-10)=-3$.

175. Answer: C)

Explanation: The factors of 12 are 1, 2, 3, 6, and 12.

176. Answer: B)

Explanation: Solving the system of equations gives $x=5$.

177. Answer: A)

Explanation: The simplified form is $5x^2-10x+3$.

178. Answer: A)

Explanation: Factoring gives $(x-2)(x-3)=0$, so the roots are $x=2$ and $x=3$.

179. Answer: A)

Explanation: The area of the triangle is $1/2 \times 5 \times 10 = 25$.

180. Answer: A)

Explanation: The potential energy (U) due to gravity is calculated using the formula $U=mgh$, where m is the mass, g is the gravitational acceleration, and hh is the height.

181. Answer: C)

Explanation: The unit of work is the Joule.

182. Answer: A)

Explanation: Ideal mechanical advantage = length / height = 10m/2m=5.

183. Answer: C)

Explanation: Impulse equals change in momentum. Since the object starts at rest, its initial momentum is zero. After gaining an impulse of 10 Ns, its momentum will be $10Ns$.

184. Answer: C)

Explanation: Bernoulli's principle describes the relationship between fluid speed and pressure.

185. Answer: C)

Explanation: Conduction is the transfer of heat through direct contact.

186. Answer: B)

Explanation: A concave lens diverges light.

187. Answer: A)

Explanation: The unit of electrical charge is the Coulomb.

188. Answer: D)

Explanation: The magnetic field inside a solenoid is described by its strength, polarity, and direction.

189. Answer: D)

Explanation: Ground effect refers to increased lift and decreased aerodynamic drag when an aircraft is close to the ground.

190. Answer: C)

Explanation: Flaperons serve to increase both lift and drag, combining the functions of flaps and ailerons.

191. Answer: B)

Explanation: Ballast is weight that is intentionally added to an aircraft to improve its balance.

192. Answer: D)

Explanation: A barrel roll is a combination of a roll and a climb, usually in the shape of a helix.

193. Answer: B)

Explanation: Inferencing involves making conclusions based on textual evidence.

194. Answer: B)

Explanation: A synonym is a word that has the same or nearly the same meaning as another word.

195. Answer: B)

Explanation: $7 \times 9 = 63$.

196. Answer: A)

Explanation: $-5 + 9 = 4$.

197. Answer: D)

Explanation: The LCM of 3 and 5 is 15.

198. Answer: A)

Explanation: Solving the system of equations gives $y = 1$.

199. Answer: A)

Explanation: The simplified form is $2x^2 + 6x + 5$.

200. Answer: B)

Explanation: The discriminant $b^2 - 4ac = (-3)^2 - 4 \times 1 \times 1 = 9 - 4 = 5$.

TEST-TAKING STRATEGIES

The **SIFT exam** can be a challenging but rewarding experience. While mastering the material is key, learning how to approach the exam strategically and managing test anxiety can make a significant difference in your performance. This section provides you with proven strategies to excel on the test, along with techniques to keep anxiety in check so you can perform your best under pressure.

Test-Taking Strategies

1. Understand the Test Format and Structure

One of the most effective ways to perform well on the SIFT exam is to familiarize yourself with the test's structure. Knowing the number of questions, the time constraints for each section, and the types of questions you will face will give you confidence and allow you to manage your time efficiently.

Action Plan:

- Review the **SIFT Exam Overview** to understand the **seven sections** (Army Aviation Information, Reading Comprehension, Mathematics Skills, Mechanical Comprehension, Spatial Apperception, and others).

- Practice each section under timed conditions to become comfortable with the pacing.

2. Time Management: Work Efficiently

The SIFT exam is **time-limited**, so you'll need to move through the questions quickly, but also accurately. The key is to **pace yourself** and not spend too much time on any single question. If you get stuck on a question, **move on and return to it later** if time allows.

Action Plan:

- Aim for a **set amount of time per question**. For example, give yourself **2 minutes per question** for the quicker sections and adjust based on the difficulty of the content.

- In the **Mechanical Comprehension** and **Mathematics Skills** sections, where problem-solving is essential, allocate more time if necessary, but don't linger too long on one question.

3. Use the Process of Elimination (POE)

When answering multiple-choice questions, if you're unsure of the correct answer, use the **Process of Elimination (POE)** to narrow down your options. Even if you can't definitively choose the right answer, eliminating one or two incorrect choices increases your chances of guessing correctly.

Action Plan:

- For every question, **eliminate the answers** you know are incorrect first. This leaves you with fewer options and helps you make a more educated guess.

4. Answer the Easy Questions First

Begin with the questions that you feel most confident about. This will help you build momentum and give you more time to focus on the harder questions later.

Action Plan:

- Quickly **scan through the test** at the beginning, marking the easy questions.

- **Answer the easy ones first**, then return to the harder questions.

5. Stay Calm and Focused

Remaining calm and focused throughout the exam will help you avoid making careless mistakes. If you find yourself getting flustered or stressed, take a **deep breath**, refocus, and remind yourself that you have prepared.

Action Plan:

- Use **deep breathing exercises** when you feel anxious: Inhale for 4 seconds, hold for 4 seconds, and exhale for 4 seconds.

- Take short **mental breaks** when you feel overwhelmed, especially between sections, to reset your focus.

6. Double-Check Your Work

If time allows, always **double-check** your answers before submitting the exam. This extra time ensures that you didn't make any simple mistakes in the heat of the moment.

Action Plan:

- If you finish early, **review your answers**—especially for sections like **Mathematics Skills** where small errors can easily occur.

- Be mindful of any skipped questions and make sure they are answered.

Overcoming Test Anxiety

Test anxiety is common, especially when preparing for an important exam like the SIFT. Fortunately, there are proven techniques to **manage** and **overcome anxiety** so it doesn't hinder your performance.

1. Prepare Thoroughly

One of the best ways to combat test anxiety is to be **well-prepared**. The more confident you feel about the material, the less anxious you will be. Make a study schedule and stick to it, using this guide to keep track of your progress.

Action Plan:

- Follow a **study plan** and track your progress each week.

- **Test yourself regularly** to identify areas of improvement, and celebrate small wins along the way.

2. Practice Under Test Conditions

Simulating actual test conditions during practice is a great way to build familiarity and reduce anxiety on test day. Time yourself during practice tests and practice in a quiet environment that mirrors the testing atmosphere.

Action Plan:

- Use **full-length practice tests** in this guide to simulate real exam conditions.

- **Take the practice tests** in a quiet, distraction-free setting to mimic the testing environment.

3. Stay Positive: Visualize Success

A positive mindset can greatly reduce anxiety. Visualization is a powerful tool that can help you feel more confident. Picture yourself successfully completing each section and achieving a high score.

Action Plan:

- **Visualize your success** before and during the test. See yourself answering questions with ease and finishing the exam confidently.

- **Affirmations**: Remind yourself that you are well-prepared and capable of succeeding.

4. Get Plenty of Rest and Eat Well

Physical preparation can contribute to mental calmness. Ensure you are well-rested before the exam and eat a balanced meal to fuel your brain. Avoid caffeine or heavy meals that might make you jittery or sluggish.

Action Plan:

- **Get 7-8 hours of sleep** the night before the exam.

- Eat a **healthy meal** that includes complex carbohydrates, lean protein, and vegetables to maintain energy.

5. Focus on the Present

It's easy to get overwhelmed by thoughts of the future or what might happen if you don't do well. Instead, focus on the **present moment**. Take each section of the test one question at a time and avoid thinking ahead to what's coming next.

Action Plan:

- **Stay present** by focusing on answering the current question to the best of your ability.

- **Take one step at a time**—focus on finishing the section at hand before worrying about the next one.

6. Take Breaks When Needed

If you feel overwhelmed during the test, **pause for a few seconds** to take a deep breath, reset, and refocus. Don't let a momentary lapse of concentration affect your entire exam.

Action Plan:

- **Use short breaks** between sections to relax your mind. Stand up, stretch, and take a few deep breaths to reduce tension.

- **Do not rush**; it's better to pace yourself and stay calm than to hurry and make mistakes.

Final Thoughts on Test-Taking and Anxiety Management

With the right test-taking strategies and effective techniques to manage anxiety, you'll be in the best possible position to excel on the SIFT exam. Remember, **preparation, focus, and a positive mindset** are your keys to success. By following the strategies and advice in this guide, you'll not only overcome test anxiety but also perform at your highest potential. Stay calm, trust in your preparation, and approach the exam with confidence!

ADDITIONAL RESOURCES

Preparing for the SIFT exam requires not only mastering the content in this study guide but also having access to additional resources that can further enhance your understanding and confidence. Below, we've compiled a list of **online resources** and **recommended academic materials** that will support your preparation and help you feel fully equipped to tackle each section of the exam.

Recommended Online Resources

1. Army Aviation Information and Aerodynamics

- **NASA's Beginner's Guide to Aerodynamics**
  Website: https://www.grc.nasa.gov
  Description: This site provides a comprehensive overview of aerodynamics, tailored for beginners. You'll find interactive simulations, diagrams, and explanations of key concepts like lift, drag, and thrust.

- **Federal Aviation Administration (FAA) Website**
  Website: https://www.faa.gov
  Description: The FAA's website contains a variety of free resources on aviation basics, flight safety, and aircraft operations. Their manuals, such as the Pilot's Handbook of Aeronautical Knowledge, can offer addition-

al insights into aviation principles.

2. Math Skills

- **Khan Academy**

  Website: https://www.khanacademy.org

  Description: Khan Academy provides free lessons on topics ranging from basic arithmetic to advanced algebra and geometry. The platform includes practice exercises and video tutorials, making it an excellent resource for reinforcing math skills.

- **Purplemath**

  Website: https://www.purplemath.com

  Description: Purplemath offers easy-to-understand explanations and step-by-step examples for algebra and geometry concepts. This site is especially useful for brushing up on core math skills and solving complex problems.

3. Mechanical Comprehension

- **Physics Classroom**

  Website: https://www.physicsclassroom.com

  Description: The Physics Classroom provides clear and accessible explanations on topics such as work, energy, electricity, and magnetism. Interactive simulations and practice problems make it an ideal resource for SIFT's Mechanical Comprehension section.

- **Engineering Toolbox**

  Website: https://www.engineeringtoolbox.com

  Description: Engineering Toolbox offers useful diagrams, formulas, and calculators for a range of physics and engineering topics. This resource can be beneficial for understanding practical applications of mechanical principles.

4. Reading Comprehension and Spatial Apperception

- **Reading Rockets**
  Website: https://www.readingrockets.org
  Description: Reading Rockets is an excellent resource for improving reading comprehension skills. It includes tips for identifying main ideas, summarizing passages, and making inferences, all of which are essential for the Reading Comprehension section.

- **Lumosity**
  Website: https://www.lumosity.com
  Description: Lumosity offers brain-training games that can help improve spatial awareness, mental rotation, and memory—all key skills for the Spatial Apperception section of the SIFT exam.

Recommended Academic Materials

1. Books on Aviation and Aerodynamics

- **"Pilot's Handbook of Aeronautical Knowledge" by the FAA**
  Description: This handbook covers the foundational concepts of aeronautics, including aerodynamics, weather, flight controls, and navigation. It is an essential reference for anyone preparing for an aviation-related exam.

- **"Fundamentals of Aerodynamics" by John D. Anderson**

Description: This textbook provides an in-depth look at the science of aerodynamics. Though more advanced, it is a valuable resource for those wanting a comprehensive understanding of aviation principles.

2. Math and Mechanical Comprehension Books

- **"Mathematics for the Trades" by Robert A. Carman**
Description: This book simplifies key math concepts needed for technical exams, including algebra, geometry, and practical applications. It's ideal for brushing up on essential skills for the Mathematics Skills section.

- **"How Things Work: The Physics of Everyday Life" by Louis A. Bloomfield**
Description: This book explains fundamental physics concepts, including mechanical and electrical principles, in an easy-to-understand way. It's an excellent supplementary text for the Mechanical Comprehension section.

3. Reading Comprehension and Spatial Skills Resources

- **"Reading Comprehension Success in 20 Minutes a Day" by LearningExpress Editors**
Description: This workbook offers practical exercises and tips for improving reading comprehension, focusing on skills like identifying main ideas and making inferences. It's great for reinforcing the strategies in this guide.

- **"Mindware Visual Puzzles: Over 300 Puzzles to Boost Brainpower"**
Description: This book includes puzzles that strengthen spatial awareness and mental rotation skills. It's an engaging resource for enhancing

spatial skills in preparation for the Spatial Apperception section.

4. Full-Length Practice Test Books

- **"SIFT Test Prep: SIFT Study Guide and Practice Test Questions for the Army Selection Instrument for Flight Training Exam" by Trivium Test Prep**
  Description: This study guide offers additional practice tests and question explanations, which can reinforce your preparation and provide a realistic exam experience.

- **"Military Flight Aptitude Tests" by Barron's Test Prep**
  Description: This book covers various military flight aptitude tests, including the SIFT. It includes practice questions, test-taking strategies, and answer explanations, making it a useful supplement to this study guide.

Final Words on Additional Resources

Preparing for the SIFT exam can be a demanding journey, but utilizing additional resources will help reinforce your understanding and enhance your confidence. These recommended online resources and academic materials are designed to provide extra practice, deeper insights, and valuable techniques for every section of the SIFT exam. Whether you're brushing up on math, diving into aerodynamics, or improving spatial awareness, these resources will equip you with the knowledge and skills needed to succeed.

Remember to integrate these resources into your study schedule, focusing on your specific areas of improvement. With consistent effort, thorough preparation, and access to quality materials, you'll be well-prepared to achieve a competitive score on the SIFT exam.

EXPLORE OUR RANGE OF STUDY GUIDES

At Test Treasure Publication, we understand that academic success requires more than just raw intelligence or tireless effort—it requires targeted preparation. That's why we offer an extensive range of study guides, meticulously designed to help you excel in various exams across the USA.

Our Offerings

- **Medical Exams:** Conquer the MCAT, USMLE, and more with our comprehensive study guides, complete with practice questions and diagnostic tests.

- **Law Exams:** Get a leg up on the LSAT and bar exams with our tailored resources, offering theoretical insights and practical exercises.

- **Business and Management Tests:** Ace the GMAT and other business exams with our incisive guides, equipped with real-world examples and scenarios.

- **Engineering & Technical Exams:** Prep for the FE, PE, and other technical exams with our specialized guides, which delve into both fundamentals and complexities.

- **High School Exams:** Be it the SAT, ACT, or AP tests, our high school range is designed to give you a competitive edge.

- **State-Specific Exams:** Tailored resources to help you with exams unique to specific states, whether it's teacher qualification exams or state civil service exams.

Why Choose Test Treasure Publication?

- **Comprehensive Coverage:** Each guide covers all essential topics in detail.

- **Quality Material:** Crafted by experts in each field.

- **Interactive Tools:** Flashcards, online quizzes, and downloadable resources to complement your study.

- **Customizable Learning:** Personalize your prep journey by focusing on areas where you need the most help.

- **Community Support:** Access to online forums where you can discuss concerns, seek guidance, and share success stories.

Contact Us

For inquiries about our study guides, or to provide feedback, please email us at support@testtreasure.com.

Order Now

Ready to elevate your preparation to the next level? Visit our website www.testtreasure.com to browse our complete range of study guides and make your purchase.

Made in United States
Troutdale, OR
04/07/2025